CIRCLING
⟊ THE ⟊
SAVANNAH

CIRCLING

~ THE ~

SAVANNAH

CULTURAL LANDMARKS OF THE
CENTRAL SAVANNAH RIVER AREA

DR. TOM MACK

Charleston   London

THE
History
PRESS

Published by The History Press
Charleston, SC 29403
www.historypress.net

Front cover, clockwise from upper right: Woodrow Wilson boyhood home, Augusta. *Tom Mack*; Banksia, Aiken. *Tom Mack*; Oakley Park, Edgefield. *Tom Mack*; Burt-Stark Mansion, Abbeville. *Michael Budd*; Barnwell County Courthouse. *Michael Budd*; Robert Mills House, Columbia. *Michael Budd*.

Back cover: Strom Thurmond Monument, Columbia. *Tom Mack*; Food storage jar, David Drake, August 24, 1857. *McKissick Museum, University of South Carolina.*

First published 2009

Manufactured in the United States

ISBN 978.1.59629.832.3

Library of Congress Cataloging-in-Publication Data

Mack, Tom.
Circling the Savannah : cultural landmarks of the central Savannah River area / Tom Mack.
p. cm.
Includes bibliographical references.
ISBN 978-1-59629-832-3
1. Historic sites--Savannah River Region (Ga. and S.C.). 2. Historic buildings--Savannah River Region (Ga. and S.C.) 3. Monuments--Savannah River Region (Ga. and S.C.) 4. Historic preservation--Savannah River Region (Ga. and S.C.) 5. Savannah River Region (Ga. and S.C.)--Description and travel. 6. Savannah River Region (Ga. and S.C.)--History, Local. 7. Savannah River Region (Ga. and S.C.)--Biography. 8. Savannah River Region (Ga. and S.C.)--Intellectual life. I. Title.
F292.S3M33 2009
975.7'9--dc22
2009039676

Contents

Contents

Acknowledgements

First of all, I would like to acknowledge the support of the administrative and editorial staff of the *Aiken Standard*, especially Scott Hunter, publisher, and Jeff Wallace, editor. I have enjoyed my long association with the paper.

Many thanks also go to my second family: the faculty and staff at the University of South Carolina–Aiken. Of particular help on this project have been Carol McKay and Troy Mothkovich.

I am grateful to Laura All and Ryan Finn at The History Press for their encouragement and guidance, and to Michael Budd, who took many of the photographs featured in this volume. His sense of adventure has made him the perfect travel companion on many of the trips chronicled in these pages.

Writing my weekly column has afforded me the opportunity to meet so many engaged and engaging individuals across our region of the country. I want to express my appreciation to all of the professional staffers and dedicated volunteers who help ensure the preservation of sites of critical importance to the history of both South Carolina and Georgia.

Introduction

For more than twenty years, I have had the pleasure of contributing a weekly column to the *Aiken Standard*. Entitled "Arts and Humanities," this column has covered a wide range of topics in a variety of disciplines but all subsumed in the broad category of cultural history.

Over those years, the individual columns devoted to regional landmarks have generally garnered the most attention, and I have received many requests to collect those texts into a single source. This volume is the answer to those reader requests. It includes thirty-six sections, most of which have appeared at one time in shorter form in the *Aiken Standard*; all of these pieces, however, have been revisited and revised to meet the requirements of this publication.

The present book is organized into four principal parts. A third of the sections are devoted to places of cultural interest in and around the city of Aiken, my base of operations for over thirty years; the other three parts include chapters on sites in Augusta and Edgefield, as well as scattered locations in Georgia and South Carolina.

In this book, I use the name Central Savannah River Area in a broader sense than intended by C.C. McCollum in 1950 when he coined the acronym CSRA to apply to a thirteen-county region of Georgia and South Carolina bisected by the Savannah River. I know that in some pieces in the final portion of the book I may have appeared to venture beyond the strict geographical boundaries encompassed by the Central Savannah River Area, but let me assure my readers that even in those chapters focused on sites in

Abbeville or Columbia, there are connections to the people and places of the CSRA.

In general, I have concentrated on landmarks within an easy driving distance from the Aiken-Augusta nexus, sites that have been hitherto largely underappreciated or about which information has not been previously synthesized for handy reference.

All in all, the sections in this book provide a very selective guide to many of the colorful people and places of this region, on both sides of the Savannah River; it is my ultimate hope that my readers will be inspired by the stories herein to go exploring and to discover more about the rich history of the Central Savannah River Area.

PART I

Aiken

AIKEN LAYS CLAIM TO ANTEBELLUM POET

At 241 Laurens Street, just above the railroad bridge, lies property once owned by one of our state's most distinguished antebellum poets. Listed on the National Historic Register as one of Aiken's oldest dwellings, the cottage was home to James Mathewes Legare, a South Carolina native who spent most of his adult years in Aiken, where he died at the age of thirty-five shortly before the outbreak of the Civil War.

Representing the sixth generation of his family in South Carolina, Legare (pronounced Le-gree) was the son of a Charleston businessman and founding editor of the farm journal *Southern Agriculturalist*. Since his father was quick to recognize the power of knowledge, James was encouraged to pursue higher education. He began his undergraduate studies at the College of Charleston and completed his bachelor's degree at St. Mary's College in Baltimore. The year he spent in the latter city may be attributed to the proximity of his influential cousin Hugh Swinton Legare, who was then in Washington serving as U.S. attorney general during the administration of President John Tyler.

Upon his return to Charleston, James Legare accepted a position as a law clerk, but his plans to become an attorney were derailed by a reversal in his father's finances and by his own deteriorating health. Legare suffered from what were termed "lung hemorrhages," perhaps symptomatic of tuberculosis. At any rate, the family left Charleston in 1846 to seek a more

The Legare-Morgan Cottage. *Tom Mack.*

healthful climate, and they presumably found what they were looking for in the hamlet of Aiken, which was then being touted for its low humidity, absence of mosquitoes and nearby restorative springs.

Not long after their resettlement, James's father John became Aiken's postmaster, and James himself engaged in a variety of enterprises, utilizing the family home as his base of operations. For a time, he used one of the rooms in the family cottage as a school for young women. The focus of the curriculum was the decorative arts, and in this regard Legare himself had something of a reputation as a sculptor and painter. In fact, one of the rooms at the Legare-Morgan Cottage still boasts three of his paintings and a mantelpiece sculpted by his hand. Painted on wood—two on narrow, vertical door panels and the third on the paneled wall between two windows—the Legare pictures may have, at one time, satisfied the general definition of *trompe l'oeil* since they are meant to replicate framed images hanging on a wall. The two paintings on door panels, for example, represent three oblong medallions suspended from a single ribbon affixed to the wall; of the three faux-framed images in each composition, the middle is the most elaborate. Despite the color change that has occurred over time, the landscapes on each central medallion are still easily recognizable as woodland scenes rendered in a twilight atmosphere.

Aiken

James Legare was in residence in Aiken when his one and only volume of poetry was published by William Ticknor of Boston in 1848. Entitled *Orta Undis* or *Sprung from Waves*, the book, whose title refers to the legend that Venus was brought forth from ocean foam, contains about thirty poems, all of which can be divided into two categories: nature and love. Since Venus was both the goddess of beauty and mother of love, Legare's choice of title seems particularly apt. Legare's work attracted the attention of poet-professor Henry Wadsworth Longfellow and South Carolina novelist William Gilmore Simms; both men considered Legare a young writer of promise.

In addition to his experimentation with the visual and literary arts, Legare fancied himself something of an inventor. In fact, he applied for at least two patents, one for a substance that he called "plastic-cotton" or "lignine." According to Curtis Davis, the author of the 1971 biography *That Ambitious Mr. Legare*, the poet-artist developed a process that "solidified the common cotton fiber" by the addition of "certain chemical agents." What resulted from this discovery was a substance that could be "molded by hand or by lathe into any shape."

Legare himself is said to have made furniture from plastic-cotton. The whereabouts of any of those particular items are currently unknown—some reports indicate that the Charleston Museum may have plastic-cotton furniture in storage—but what is certain is that one of the mantelpieces in the Legare-Morgan Cottage is molded of "lignine." This fanciful composition features a grimacing male face framed by rococo swirls, curves and volutes; an infant stretches across the man's brow, its legs astride the nose. According to at least one observer, these central figures are meant to dramatize the birth of Athena, the goddess of wisdom said to have sprung from the brow of Zeus. Given James Legare's classical education, this is certainly a reasonable hypothesis.

Unfortunately, because of his lack of capital, Legare was never able to exploit the full potential of his inventions—in addition to plastic-cotton, he is reported to have created a variety of color-permeated encaustic tile. In fact, at the time of his death in 1859, Legare was in the process of requesting investment funds from James Henry Hammond of Redcliffe Plantation in Beech Island—as the principal landowner in the area and a former South Carolina governor and U.S. senator, Hammond was often seen as a potential financier.

Thus, as fate would have it, Legare died in genteel poverty, and he was buried in a grave that remained unmarked until 1942. In that year, a monument to Legare's memory was erected in the churchyard of Saint

The grave site of James Legare. *Tom Mack.*

Thaddeus Episcopal Church on Pendleton Street; the cost of this stone marker was underwritten by individual donations from numerous Aiken High School students. In the same plot are buried Legare's parents and his wife Anne.

The poet's former residence endures on a verdant lot, and walking on the grounds even today, one can readily imagine how the site may once have inspired Legare's composition in both word and image. His poem entitled "Haw-Blossoms," for example, begins: "While yester evening through the vale descending from my cottage door I strayed, how cool and fresh the look all nature wore." On this particular stroll, Legare singles out for praise native plants like the "calmia" or "kalmia" growing on "cliff-sides inaccessible" and the haw or white hawthorn with its "meek blossoms" and fruit "purple ripe and red."

As a poet in the Romantic tradition, Legare responded to the lessons he found inherent in the natural world; the plants that he featured in his poetry—the "jasmines in December" and the laurel blossoms in May—still speak eloquently of his life and the early history of Aiken.

NOVEL HIGHLIGHTS AIKEN'S ROLE IN CIVIL WAR

In his critically acclaimed novel *The March*, published in 2005, E.L. Doctorow uses his now trademark blend of fact and fiction to re-create and interpret for a modern audience Union general William Tecumseh Sherman's momentous invasion of Georgia and the Carolinas in 1864–65.

Divided into three sections corresponding to the three states through which Sherman made his devastating way—Georgia, South Carolina and North Carolina—the novel sweeps the reader along with the conquering army, which Doctorow compares to an omnivorous creature with "a great segmented body moving in contractions and dilations at a rate of 12 or 15 miles a day." Each of the sixty thousand troops under General Sherman's command "has no identity but as a cell in the body of this giant creature's function, which is to move forward and consume all before it."

Of particular interest to area residents, however, will be Doctorow's use of Union cavalry officer Hugh Judson Kilpatrick as a significant character in his evolving narrative. A principal player in what is now known as the Battle of Aiken, the hunchbacked Kilpatrick was one of the most colorful and controversial participants in Sherman's invasion of the Deep South, and Doctorow takes full advantage of some of the general's more vivid traits. Kilpatrick was, for example, a man who relished physical pleasure, and we see him in one scene making a narrow escape in his underwear from a Confederate raid on a farmhouse outside of Fayetteville, North Carolina, where he was "entertaining" a young woman who had attached herself to his division composed of cavalry and mounted infantry.

In another scene, this one set in Allendale, Kilpatrick drafts, on the spot, a Creole chef who had once cooked for a prosperous Southern family but now would be his personal "Sergeant of the Mess." It is while he enjoys a dinner devised by his new cook that the town of Barnwell (dubbed "Burnwell" by Kilpatrick) is set on fire. Kilpatrick and his officers eat their fill, dance and womanize while most of the town goes up in flames.

Not much later in the novel, however, the reckless General Kilpatrick experiences a temporary setback to his largely unopposed advance through South Carolina; this comes in Aiken. Although Doctorow devotes less than two pages to the cavalry engagement that took place in what is now the heart of the city's downtown area—he does not identify the battle itself until fifteen pages later in the text—the author does manage to capture much of the disorientation of the riders caught in this "roiling entanglement of blue and gray."

As seen through the eyes of a Union signal officer named Morrison, who delivers a message from Sherman to Kilpatrick and finds himself subsequently and rather reluctantly part of an ill-fated foray into the town, this short section is one of the most vivid battle sequences in the book.

Each year, like Doctorow's character Morrison, members of the general public have a chance to serve as eyewitnesses to history or at least a skillful reenactment of the same as Civil War enthusiasts from far and wide converge on Aiken to re-create this battle during which Kilpatrick's men were repulsed by Confederate cavalry under the command of General Joe Wheeler. According to some estimates, more than fifteen thousand people attend some part of this popular "living history" presentation annually. Thus, what Kilpatrick originally characterized in his dispatch to Sherman as an informal plan to "make demonstrations toward Augusta," at which the Confederacy's largest munitions factory was located, has become over time and with considerable reinvention the inspiration for one of South Carolina's biggest tourist events.

The original battle took place in downtown Aiken, with Kilpatrick's forces advancing along Park, Richland and Barnwell Avenues, and the fiercest fighting is said to have occurred around what is now the First Baptist Church. Indeed, at the corner of Richland Avenue and York Street, a local memorial association erected a stone marker in 1911 to commemorate the "Confederate soldiers who lost their lives in defense of Aiken, February 11, 1865." On the other side of the sanctuary are stones marking the graves of

Graves of Union Soldiers. *Tom Mack.*

twenty Union soldiers; sixteen carry individual names—some of these, like Driscoll and Massey and Sweitzer, can still be read—and the inscription "5th US Cavalry." The remaining four are marked simply "Union soldier."

The re-created battle takes place each year just north of town, on Powell Pond Road off Route 19 just south of the intersection with Interstate 20. Established and maintained with the aid of admission fees and donations, the Brigadier General Barnard E. Bee Confederate Memorial Park may very well be the only site—it can certainly claim to be the largest—in the country dedicated primarily to historical reenactment. For more information, visit www.battleofaiken.org.

AIKEN COUNTY MUSEUM
REVEALS TREASURES INSIDE AND OUT

For the general public, the Aiken County Historical Museum offers the best glimpse of the city in its heyday as a winter resort. Housed in one of the most notable "cottages" built by the jet set of an earlier age, the museum showcases a wide range of historical artifacts in a building that is itself a treasure of the past.

In 1931, on a 3.5-acre lot that he purchased at the bottom of Laurens Street, Richard Howe decided to build a winter retreat. A New Yorker and former executive of International Harvester—he had married into the Deering family, co-founders of the company—Howe commissioned noted architect Willis Irvin to expand the existing nineteenth-century residence, a wooden structure of 3,500 square feet, by incorporating a 14,000-square-foot addition. In essence, the brick addition eventually housed the main rooms, and the original structure came to serve ancillary purposes, including space for live-in servants.

Willis Irvin, who designed many local landmarks, including the remodeled Aiken County Courthouse and what is now the Green Boundary Club, provided Howe with a residence of consummate grace and charm. According to Elliott Levy, the museum's executive director since 2006, it may very well be thanks to the building's elegant neoclassical features—such as the seven arched doorways leading off the main entrance and the intricate dentil moldings in the beautifully proportioned formal drawing room—that

Banksia/Aiken County Historical Museum. *Tom Mack.*

Aiken

Banksia, named for the little yellow roses that grew on the serpentine walls surrounding the estate, eventually became the beneficiary of an aesthetic halo effect.

Indeed, despite its varied incarnations after the family sold the house in 1951, so much of the original fabric of the building remains to this day. This survival is all the more remarkable when one considers that it served consecutively as a boardinghouse for workers at the Savannah River Site, a campus for both Southern Methodist University and the University of South Carolina–Aiken and a public library until it assumed its current identity as the county historical museum in 1989.

One of the most enjoyable features of any visit to the museum is pausing in one's ramble through the labyrinth of rooms—the original Howe residence was composed of nearly fifty rooms, including fifteen bathrooms—to consult the vintage photographs by Tebbs-Knell, Incorporated, a photographic firm from New York City, mounted here and there on the walls. These framed images, similar to ones that Tebbs-Knell contributed to the landmark 1931 volume entitled *Southern Architecture Illustrated*, show the interior spaces as they appeared in the 1930s, and it is fascinating to compare how the rooms looked just after the house was built and how they look now.

Other echoes of the residence's gilded past are the carefully manicured grounds, which are in a perpetual state of active and planned renewal, and the vestiges of equine activity. In the latter category is a concrete mounting block placed just off the circular drive. Bearing the date 1932 and the footprints of two of Richard Howe's granddaughters, the block was used for getting up on a horse. In keeping with the equestrian activities with which Aiken is famously associated, Howe kept a stable of horses.

Besides the building itself, which may be considered the museum's largest artifact, the current facility is the repository of a host of items that recount the story of Aiken County. Of the many exhibits, Elliott Levy is perhaps most proud of what is now called the County Room, which traces the history of the area from the time of Fort Moore, built in 1715 on the South Carolina side of the Savannah River just south of Augusta, to the period of Reconstruction—Aiken County was carved out of four counties in 1871 by an act of the state legislature then dominated by Radical Republicans and their supporters.

A longtime favorite of museum visitors in general is the space in the original frame section of the building now devoted to the Moody Drugstore. According to Joyce Ross, who directed the museum in 1984 when it shared space at Banksia with the public library, the store was once a landmark in the town of Dunbarton, which vanished from the map in 1952 to make way for the Savannah River Site, a federal facility for the processing of nuclear materials. Henry Moody boxed up the contents of his store, furniture and all, and stored everything away in a barn for thirty-two years until donating the full contents of his old business to the museum. Today it serves as a time capsule from the middle of the last century.

The museum itself is anything but a time capsule. In fact, its walls continually reverberate with activity: concerts, special lectures and meetings of local groups. Since assuming the directorship, Elliott Levy has made a concerted effort to establish the museum as a center of community activity, and the hospitality that was the hallmark of Richard Howe's early residency continues today in the museum's engaging exhibits and the welcoming spirit of its staff. For additional information, visit the Aiken County Historical Museum on the web at www.aikencountysc.gov/tourism/museum.htm.

HOPELAND GARDENS LINKED TO RACING CONTROVERSY

For winter's rains and ruins are over,
And all the season of snows and sins;
The days dividing lover and lover,
The light that loses, the night that wins;
And in green underwood and cover
Blossom by blossom the spring begins.

So reads one passage from the verse drama *Atalanta in Calydon* by the nineteenth-century English poet Algernon Charles Swinburne. Although his interest in the coming of spring stemmed largely from his desire to provide a setting for his retelling of Greek legend, Swinburne struck a responsive chord in all readers longing for the end of winter and the coming of the spring.

There is perhaps no better place in Aiken to celebrate the time of the year when plants revive than Hopeland Gardens. With the return of warmer weather, it is always a treat to wander the garden's network of paved and sandy paths, sheltered by century-old live oaks.

These public gardens off Whiskey Road were once the private estate of the Iselin family, and many of the remaining landmarks on the site still hearken back to the time of the wealthy northerners who once called Aiken their winter home. The park's three central fountains, for example, were placed in the foundation of the former Iselin residence, and the Aiken Garden Club now uses as its reference library the playhouse where the Iselin children once spent many happy hours.

Although most public information about this most notable Aiken attraction makes reference to the fact that it was Hope Goddard Iselin, the widow of C. Oliver Iselin, who bequeathed her family's fourteen-acre estate to the city in 1970, little more is commonly known about the Iselins other than that simple fact. Indeed, there is much more to the Iselin story than a widow's public generosity, however far-reaching that has proven to be.

The heir to a large fortune amassed by his grandfather, who invested in railroads and coal mines, Charles Oliver Iselin dedicated his leisure hours to boating on a very important scale. In fact, after his election to the New York Yacht Club in 1877, Iselin found himself a major player in one of the world's most significant sporting events, the America's Cup.

The origin of this international race can be traced to 1851 and the Great Exhibition at the Crystal Palace in London. As part of this event organized by Prince Albert to show off the cultural and technological dominance of the British Empire in the nineteenth century, an impromptu race around the Isle of Wight was held between an American boat and a host of British yachts. Financed by the New York Yacht Club, the American yacht won, against all odds. The silver cup accorded the winner of this competition was subsequently named for the American schooner *America*, and eventually a circular room was built to showcase the cup at the yacht club's headquarters in central Manhattan.

For 132 years, the longest winning streak in sporting history, the New York Yacht Club defended the trophy against all challengers. In fact, from 1851 to 1983, there were twenty-five unsuccessful challenges by competitors from other nations. Among the most famous were the five successive Shamrock challenges mounted by Irish tea baron Sir William Lipton between 1899 and 1930. Although he lost all five attempts to wrest the cup from its American defenders, Lipton shrewdly used his multiple campaigns to advertise his tea, which became one of the world's most popular commercial brands.

Charles Oliver Iselin's active involvement with the America's Cup began in 1893, when he led the syndicate that built the yacht *Vigilant*, chosen to represent the New York Yacht Club in the race of that year, and extended to the first two of the Lipton challenges in 1899 and 1903. Mrs. Iselin is said to have been particularly attached to the 1899 racing vessel *Columbia*, and she is

The bust of Hope Goddard Iselin. *Tom Mack.*

reported to have joined her husband onboard for each of his many voyages during the yachting season of that year. It is also said that she served as the first female crew member on a final run for the coveted trophy.

The greatest threat to Iselin's triumphant management of a series of America's Cup competitive yachts came in 1895 when Lord Dunraven, who captained the British yacht *Valkyrie III*, launched a series of protests because he suspected that the American yacht's ballast had been altered. Designed by Nathaniel Herreshoff, the American-built *Defender* was among the earliest sailing boats to sport a keel of enormous depth slung beneath a shallow hull. Even though he generously offered to repeat the entire match, a full inquiry of the matter exonerated Iselin, who had led the *Defender* campaign; Dunraven, who refused to apologize for his mistake, has since been regarded as a model of poor sportsmanship.

Thus, it is interesting to note that even though Hopeland Gardens today plays host to the Thoroughbred Racing Hall of Fame, a shrine to Aiken's many contributions to equestrian sports, the property was originally owned by a family whose name is synonymous with yacht racing.

Besides the many features added to the public complex by the City of Aiken in recent years, a portrait bust of Hope Goddard Iselin was unveiled in 2006. Created by Maria Kirby-Smith, an internationally recognized figurative sculptor based in Camden, South Carolina, the bronze sculpture depicts Mrs. Iselin, meticulously coifed, radiantly smiling and in the prime of life.

This is a fitting tribute to the woman who left her mark on sporting history and bequeathed the gardens to the citizens of her adopted town for their "pleasure and enjoyment." For additional information, visit Hopeland Gardens on the web at www.cityofaikensc.gov.

AIKEN MONUMENTS MEMORIALIZE THE "LOST CAUSE"

So keen was the frustration and despair of Confederate supporters at the end of the Civil War that many sought consolation by romanticizing their defeat, by turning their military loss into a kind of moral victory. Adherents of what eventually became known as the "Lost Cause" argued that it was better to fight bravely in defense of a noble ideal—in this case, states' rights—no matter how overwhelming the odds than to submit humbly to Northern aggression.

In the decades following the war, this notion of the Lost Cause acquired momentum, and across the American South, monuments were erected to those who gave their lives for the Confederacy, a group of warriors now popularly perceived as chivalric defenders of the old order. Many of these

The Aiken County Confederate Monument. *Tom Mack.*

memorials were financed by public subscription in campaigns orchestrated by local women's organizations, often dominated by the widows and orphaned daughters of soldiers lost in the war.

Such is the case with the Aiken County Confederate Monument, the centerpiece of the traffic circle at the intersection of Park and Chesterfield

Streets. It took nine years for the Ladies Monument Association of Aiken to raise the funds to purchase the twenty-foot granite obelisk, which was dedicated in a public ceremony on July 23, 1901.

The base is embellished with text. On the side facing the Aiken County Courthouse is a passage from a speech by Ellison Capers, a former Confederate general who eventually became the bishop of the Episcopal Diocese of South Carolina. Capers himself was a major proponent of the concept of the Lost Cause; according to Walter Edgar, the author of *South Carolina: A History*, "[S]eldom was there an important Confederate observance of any kind in which the soldier-bishop did not participate." In this case, the principal inscription on the Aiken County Confederate Monument is taken from Capers: "They gave their all in defense of home, honor, liberty, and the independence of their native land. They fought the patriots' fight. They kept the faith of their fathers. Forever honored and forever mourned."

Capers's patriotic assertion is in keeping with one of the principal arguments used in defense of the Confederate cause, which held that the recent war was, in essence, a continuation of the American Revolution, a logical evolutionary step in the struggle against tyranny. It is, therefore, no mere coincidence that the obelisk—which had been chosen even before the Civil War as the design of the national memorial for the country's first president and the commander-in-chief of American forces during the Revolutionary War—should become a popular shape for monuments commemorating the Confederate dead.

Carved on the base of the Aiken obelisk facing north is the date of the unveiling, an acknowledgment of the contribution of the Ladies Monument Association of Aiken and the simple dedication: "In loving tribute to the Confederate Soldiers of Aiken County."

On all four sides on the top of the plinth upon which the obelisk rests are military symbols: a cannon, crossed rifles, crossed swords and a warship. Two of these images offer interesting variations on more traditional renderings. The silhouette of the warship, for example, is clearly meant to replicate the outline of the CSS *Virginia*, the ironclad vessel built from the remains of the USS *Merrimack*. This reconfigured Confederate warship engaged the USS *Monitor* in the first naval battle featuring two armored vessels; the Battle of Hampton Roads ended in a draw.

Of even greater interest is the fact that the image of the crossed swords is overlaid with a laurel wreath, emblematic of victory since ancient times. This particular juxtaposition is characteristic of the iconography of the

The Seigler Memorial. *Tom Mack.*

Lost Cause and its assertion that the South's defeat in the Civil War was actually a triumph of honor.

Another notable memorial in the city of Aiken that dates from the early twentieth century and similarly embodies the philosophical stance represented in the Confederate monument is the Seigler Memorial in Bethany Cemetery at the top of Laurens Street. Crowned with a full-figure stone sculpture of a Confederate soldier, this impressive structure marks the grave of Aquilla Seigler, who died in 1906 but wanted to be remembered primarily for his service as a young captain during the Civil War.

The base of the monument indicates that Seigler fought with the Twenty-second South Carolina Infantry, which saw action throughout the war, starting with Second Manassas and ending with Petersburg and Appomattox. Although his wife and two of his children are buried in plots contiguous to his, the monument of the soldier dominates the grave site; they all rest in the shadow of the soldier-hero who, according to the inscription on the plinth, "has gone from labor to refreshment and has crossed over the river to rest with his comrades."

Across the South, in towns large and small, public and private monuments were erected in memory of the soldiers who, in the words of South Carolina legislator and United States diplomat William Henry Trescot, "glorified a fallen cause by the simple manhood of their lives, the patient endurance of suffering, and the heroism of death."

PICKENS-SALLEY HOUSE
CELEBRATES TWO GREAT WOMEN

By the time it was moved to the campus of the University of South Carolina–Aiken in three parts in 1989, the Pickens-Salley House had already borne witness to almost two centuries of southern history. Now it serves as much-needed space for administrative offices and public receptions, but in the past, the Pickens-Salley House was home to two extraordinary women, Lucy Holcombe Pickens and Eulalie Chafee Salley.

Born in Tennessee in 1832 but raised in what was then the Republic of Texas, Lucy Holcombe was sent to a finishing school in Bethlehem, Pennsylvania, for two years before she returned to her father's plantation to become the object of a host of potential suitors. She eventually married the twice-widowed Francis Wilkinson Pickens, a South Carolina landowner and politician who was twenty-two years older than she.

Grandson of Andrew Pickens, Revolutionary War hero, and son of Andrew Pickens Jr., South Carolina's governor from 1816 to 1818, Francis Pickens appeared destined for a life in politics, serving as a member of the United States Congress before being elected governor of South Carolina on the eve of the Civil War.

Between those two periods in elected office, however, Pickens spent three years in Russia as our country's ambassador to the court of Czar Alexander II. The time spent in St. Petersburg was particularly eventful for Lucy Pickens, who became a personal favorite of the royal family. The czar adopted her as a regular dancing partner, and both the czar and czarina served as godparents to Lucy's only child, a daughter nicknamed Douschka, or Little Darling, born in Russia in 1858.

The excitement of foreign travel, however, was followed by the turmoil of national politics when the couple and their newborn child returned to South Carolina in the fall of 1860 and Francis Pickens became almost immediately embroiled in gubernatorial electioneering. As governor, he supported secession; he is also credited with having approved the first military engagement of the Civil War: firing upon the relief ship *Star of the West* that was bringing supplies to Major Robert Anderson's besieged garrison at Fort Sumter in Charleston harbor.

Lucy Pickens also ardently served what came to be known as the Lost Cause. In 1861, the so-called Holcombe Legion was first assembled; these seven companies of infantry and one of cavalry were said to have been personally financed by Lucy Pickens from the sale of jewels lavished on her by the Russian

Confederate currency featuring Lucy Pickens, 1864.

royal family. For this generous act and as a tribute to her celebrated beauty, Confederate treasury secretary Christopher Memminger featured a likeness of Lucy Pickens on the 1862 $1 bill and the 1862, 1863 and 1864 $100 bills. Because of this latter distinction, Lucy eventually became popularly known as the "Queen of the Confederacy."

After his term of office ended in 1862—South Carolina governors served terms of only two years until the state constitution was amended in 1926 to permit a four-year term—Francis, then in ill health, retired to the family plantation, Edgewood, in Edgefield County, where he died in 1869, bearing witness to the devastation of his home state and the loss of much of his property—particularly his plantations in Mississippi and Alabama. Lucy, who outlived him by thirty years, managed to preserve Edgewood by selling off some personal valuables, trying to make the plantation a profitable agricultural enterprise and plying her pen.

The rambling frame house on the outskirts of Edgefield, however, was deserted by the 1920s, when Eulalie Salley attended a picnic in its barren rooms. Named after her mother, who had been christened Eulalie in honor of the "gentle" and "bright-eyed" title character in a poem by Edgar Allan Poe, Marguerite Eulalie Chafee II was born in Augusta in 1883 but was raised in Aiken. At the age of twenty-three, she married Julian B. Salley, a local lawyer.

Despite what her husband saw as her responsibilities as his wife and the mother of their two small children, Eulalie listened to the beat of her own drummer. To her husband's dismay and the ridicule of many of her contemporaries, for example, she established the Aiken Equal Suffrage League in 1913. Eulalie Salley was in the forefront of the fight for passage of the Nineteenth Amendment, which was ratified in 1920 but not officially sanctioned by South Carolina until almost fifty years later. On that fateful day in 1969, at the age of eighty-five, she was a special guest of the General Assembly in the statehouse in Columbia.

A professional woman long before such a personal choice was accepted by the members of polite society, Eulalie became a licensed realtor in 1915 and soon established a reputation for unparalleled customer service. "We do everything but brush your teeth," she once observed to a prospective client.

Eulalie Salley purchased Edgewood in 1929 and had the house moved to a fifteen-acre site on Kalmia Hill. In subsequent years, she embellished the walls with museum-quality woodwork—some of the hand-carved

The Pickens-Salley House. *Tom Mack.*

wainscoting and cornices were purchased from an eighteenth-century home on Ladies Island—and filled the interiors with carefully selected antiques; she was able to reacquire a crystal chandelier reputedly presented to Lucy Pickens by the Russian czar.

Today, the Pickens-Salley House provides office space for various administrative operations on the USCA campus. The house and its grounds have also served as the backdrop for many community-related social events, and it pleases me to think that both Lucy Pickens—the ghost of Lucy is said to haunt the east wing of the house still—and Eulalie Salley would take comfort in the fact that the home that they so loved still serves an important public function and still provides pleasure to countless citizens.

AIKEN BOASTS MASTERPIECE
OF RELIGIOUS ART

Impressive are the vestiges of Aiken's glory days as a winter resort. The Aiken County Historical Museum is housed in Banksia, the former winter home of millionaire Richard Howe, and the city is the grateful beneficiary of a public garden that was once Hopeland, the fourteen-acre estate of the Iselin family.

In addition to buildings and grounds, however, the wealthy northerners who came to Aiken to spend the winter left behind at least one extraordinary work of fine art. In a chamber just off the vestibule of Saint Mary Help of Christians Catholic Church on Park Avenue is Gustave Dore's sculpture entitled *Virgin and Child*. This is a little-known masterpiece by a major nineteenth-century artist.

How did this work find its way to Aiken? Apparently Harry La Montagne, a former winter resident of Aiken, saw the sculpture in Paris, where it won third prize in an international competition in 1880. He purchased the piece and brought it to America as a gift for his wife. Their daughter, Beatrice La Montagne, subsequently presented the sculpture to Monsignor Smith, then rector of St. Mary's, in 1947.

The life-size bronze depicts the Virgin Mary holding the Christ child. Unlike most traditional depictions of the Madonna and infant—which often show a seated Virgin with the child on her lap or standing near her side—the Dore sculpture opts for a full, standing figure of the Virgin with her head bent to touch the face of her child. Her expression is one of tender, maternal concern.

Gustave Dore's *Virgin and Child. Tom Mack.*

The figure of the child is more suspended than supported by his mother's embrace. His little arms are outstretched as a possible prefiguring of the crucifixion. It can be argued that the child has already accepted a fate far beyond the reach of his mother's pensive solicitude.

In this way, the sculpture is an interesting merging of the two customary Madonna and child treatments: the mother and infant and also the mother and adult son. We know the latter pose of Mary and the crucified Christ as the "pieta" grouping, from the Italian word for both "pity" and "piety." Dore has managed to combine in his treatment both the joyousness and hope of childhood and a foreshadowing of adult sacrifice.

The work was cast in the foundry of the Thiebaut brothers, and it bears their mark on the base; it is also signed by the artist "G-Dore." Gustave Dore (1833–1883) is best remembered today as a book illustrator; his wood-engraved illustrations for such works as Dante's *Divine Comedy*, Cervantes's *Don Quixote*, Milton's *Paradise Lost* and the Bible were very popular and much imitated in his day. Without a formal art education, Dore was self-supporting by the age of sixteen because of the success of his drawings and caricatures for magazines and books; these illustrations numbered over ten thousand by the time of his death. Dore was so prolific, in fact, that at one time he employed more than forty block-cutters.

However, Dore was concerned even more about his reputation as a painter and a sculptor. He created enormous canvases based on historical and Biblical events; they appealed to the nineteenth-century penchant for morally edifying subjects and apparently succeeded in meeting even the severe demands of Queen Victoria, who purchased one of Dore's paintings. A number of American museums also possess Dore canvases, including the Art Institute of Chicago and the National Gallery of Art in Washington, D.C.

These works also exhibited another hallmark of Dore's style: his love of drama. Perhaps his best-known sculpture, for instance, is the figure of D'Artagnan seated at the base of the monument to Alexandre Dumas in the Place Malesherbes in Paris. This character from *The Three Musketeers* is captured in a rare moment of repose, one arm on his hip and his sword across one knee. Critics call Dore's style "Romantic Realism" because it blends realistic detail with theatrical intention.

Certainly some of this flavor is captured in the St. Mary's sculpture. The piece combines both the image of maternal love realistically rendered, from the elegant draperies to the finely molded features, and also a dramatic foretelling of the ultimate sacrifice of the cross. Dore is said to have been very close to his own mother, and perhaps some of that filial devotion motivated his creation of this sculpture.

Thanks to the generosity of local residents, Dick and Rita Schmidt, the chamber dedicated to the display of the Dore sculpture was recently renovated. The walls are now painted a forest green over which is stenciled a diamond-shaped design featuring fleur-de-lis, crosses and what appear to be dogwood blossoms. These three emblems successfully echo the sculpture's transatlantic heritage, from its creation in France to its final home in the American South.

Aiken can certainly be proud of its rich history and those tangible remnants of the past that still remain. Among the town's greatest treasures, one that deserves special notice is certainly the Dore sculpture at Saint Mary Help of Christians Catholic Church.

CELEBRATED PIANIST
ONCE CALLED AIKEN HOME

When I first arrived in Aiken in the late 1970s, I rented an apartment in a complex now converted to condominiums on Laurens Street between Colleton and South Boundary. Little did I know at the time that my temporary home was on the site of the former residence of one of the greatest pianists of the twentieth century.

Indeed, it was not until 1985 that a historical marker was placed "several hundred feet west" of the spot where once stood the three-story home of Josef Hofmann. Born in Podgorze, near Krakow, Poland, in 1876, Hofmann became a professional pianist at the age of nine, impressing Franz Liszt, Camille Saint-Saëns and Anton Rubinstein. When he was only eleven, in 1887, this child prodigy recorded several cylinders on Thomas Edison's new recording machine; these recordings, since lost, were the first in history according to some scholars.

Josef Hofmann's international concert career took him, in 1904, to Aiken for a recital at Joye Cottage, the winter home of wealthy New York businessman and former U.S. secretary of the navy William C. Whitney. It was at this event that he met Marie Eustis, the woman who was to become his wife. Belonging to a prominent family who, along with the Hitchcocks, can be credited with making Aiken a great winter resort, Marie Eustis was divorced from her first husband and eleven years older than Hofmann. Neither was to know, on that singular night, that they would soon be drawn to each other and would marry one year later.

Their marriage had its complications. The Eustis family disapproved of the match because they felt that the itinerant life of a concert pianist was inappropriate for a woman of Marie's upbringing. It was said that the couple had nothing in common but music. "And love," Marie Hofmann would add.

The Hofmanns eventually bought an Aiken home, which they called Fermata after the musical term for "stop" or "rest." Regardless of Josef's demanding professional travel, they always spent Christmas at their Aiken residence. During the early years of their marriage, Marie accompanied Josef on tour, and extensive excerpts from her Russian and Mexican travel diaries are featured in the 1965 Graydon and Sizemore double biography entitled *The Amazing Marriage*. Hofmann was particularly popular in Russia prior to the Bolshevik Revolution. Records indicate, for example, that in St. Petersburg in 1912 he played twenty-one consecutive sold-out concerts, during which he never repeated a single piece but, thanks to his phenomenal memory, performed 255 different works.

Josef Hofmann.
Theodore Presser Company.

Aiken

Eventually, however, Marie spent less time with her husband on his travels and more time in Aiken because she wanted to be with their daughter Josefa, and in 1919 she founded the Fermata School for Girls on the third floor of the Hofmann home on Laurens Street. In 1921, due to the success of the venture, the school was moved to a nine-acre estate on Whiskey Road, the present site of the Fermata Club.

The year 1927 proved a turning point in Hofmann's marriage and career. It was during that year that Marie granted him a divorce so that he could marry Elizabeth Short, a woman thirty years his junior with whom he had been carrying on an affair. It was also in 1927 that he assumed the directorship of the Curtis Institute of Music in Philadelphia and slowly turned the fledgling institution into one of the best music conservatories in the world. Ever since he studied with Anton Rubenstein in Dresden, Germany, Hofmann had been interested in music education, and he wrote from 1901 to 1912 a popular column entitled "Piano Questions" for the magazine *Ladies Home Journal*. Many of these instructional tips were later collected in a 1920 volume entitled *Piano Playing with Piano Questions*.

As director of the Curtis Institute, Hofmann believed in the highest standards; he wanted to have only the most talented students taught by the greatest musical artists. In support of this goal, he was able to procure an enormous endowment for the school, which made it possible to provide free tuition and travel to his students and to pay his stellar faculty high wages. Unfortunately, Hofmann was able to devote his undivided attention to the school for only about six years (1927 to 1933). From 1933 until his resignation in 1938, he resumed his annual tours abroad; a combination of absenteeism and the financial pressures of the Great Depression resulted in his eventually losing the confidence of the school's trustees.

In 1939, Hofmann moved his second family to California, where he retired from the concert stage in 1946 and died in 1957. During his years on the West Coast, it is said that he spent more time on his inventions than on his music. Over his lifetime, he acquired over sixty patents, mostly for automobile parts, including a new kind of shock absorber and what may have been the first windshield wiper.

It is as a pianist, however, that Hofmann remains a legend. According to his own admission, Sergei Rachmaninoff had only one photograph of another pianist in his music room, and that was a portrait of Hofmann. In fact, the celebrated Russian composer dedicated his third piano concerto to Hofmann, whose keyboard mastery he considered equal to his own.

In the last few decades, due to increasingly sophisticated audio technology, a number of Hofmann's early recordings and concert tapes have been released on CD. The third release in the Nimbus Records *Grand Piano* series, for example, is devoted to nine Chopin selections recorded by Hofmann between 1920 and 1926. Marston Records has also released eight CDs devoted to Josef Hofmann's recordings and taped recitals.

FREE-SPIRITED WRITER LED TRANSATLANTIC LIFE

"She reads a story from a book; I lie in bed and hear the words sing in the darkness like great birds," wrote Gamel Woolsey in her poem "All That the Child Remembers Now." This work chronicles the poet's childhood memories of life at Breeze Hill Plantation outside of Aiken, where she was born in 1899.

Although her future was to take her far from her southern roots, Gamel Woolsey continued to romanticize her childhood in Aiken and adolescence in Charleston, and she never adjusted to the changes that this century brought to the South. In 1951, for instance, when she returned from Spain to Aiken after her brother's death, Woolsey saw the start of the town's continuing construction and population boom, and she was disturbed by all the hustle and bustle.

According to Lynne Rhodes, a member of the English faculty at the University of South Carolina–Aiken and an expert on the poet's life and work, Gamel Woolsey had an "instinct for retreating" into her own personal past and into the collective past of what she saw as the "Eden-like" region of her birth.

The daughter of New York banker William Woolsey, who had moved to Aiken in 1871 because of the town's reputation as a winter health resort, and Charleston socialite Bessie Gammell, Elsa "Gamel" Woolsey lived what appears to have been an idyllic childhood of riding horses, reading books and daydreaming. Even after she moved with her family to her mother's home in Charleston following her father's death when she was ten, Gamel Woolsey never cut her emotional ties to Aiken because of happy memories of her youth and the abiding presence of relatives in this area.

In 1923, as a young adult, Woolsey moved to New York with dreams of becoming an actress or a visual artist, but nothing much ever came of either ambition. As influences that may have contributed to Gamel Woolsey's indolence as an adult, Lynne Rhodes points to an essential passivity inherited from her mother and to her own chronically delicate health attributable to an early struggle with tuberculosis.

Rhodes asserts that it was this passivity that "always inspired others to protect her." Coupled with her physical beauty, this trait brought her the attention of male admirers, and Gamel Woolsey had a number of significant love relationships: an early marriage to New Zealand journalist Rex Hunter, a long-standing affair with the English novelist Llewellyn Powys and a forty-year relationship with the writer Gerald Brenan.

Powys carried on a transatlantic affair with Gamel Woolsey for years even though he was married to the feminist editor Alyse Gregory at the time. Even after she moved in with Gerald Brenan, both Powys and Woolsey maintained their emotional bond. The character of Dittany Stone in Powys's novel *Love and Death* is modeled after Gamel Woolsey, and a book of his letters to her was published in 1973 under the title *So Wild a Thing*. Her own fictionalized account of her quest to find a soul mate is chronicled in the novel *One Way of Love*, which was published posthumously in 1987 by Virago Modern Classics; herein, the romantic longings of the character Mariana mirrors those of Woolsey herself.

Gamel Woolsey. *Pythia Press.*

As the mate of Gerald Brenan—they considered themselves married although she was never legally divorced from Hunter—Gamel eventually lived in Spain and published two

Breeze Hill Plantation. *Tom Mack.*

volumes based on her residence in that country: *Death's Other Kingdom*, an account of the civil war in the 1930s—the book was reprinted in America in 1998 under the title *Malaga is Burning*—and a book of Spanish fairy tales.

Her most significant work published during her lifetime was *Middle Earth*, a collection of thirty-nine poems. Lynne Rhodes argues that the twin themes of the book are Gamel Woolsey's "romantic view of childhood and her experience with sexual love." This can also be said to have been the summarizing essence of her relationship with Llewellyn Powys. Both shared "an imaginative, secret world" that glorified childhood memories and their own physical attraction for each other. Her poems "All That the Child Remembers Now" and "For the Flesh" appeared in this volume; they objectify this desire to freeze time either through memory or through love. "Is there a third way through the wilderness?" she wrote, "A place to where the heart went, where the past is folded closely in a little space?"

Aiken County maintains ties to this fascinating woman and lyrical writer since ownership of Breeze Hill Plantation on Banks Mill Road is still retained by the Woolsey/Fliflet family. Once noted for its cattle-breeding and cotton-producing operations, the five-hundred-acre plantation is now used primarily for the boarding of horses. The main house was torn down during the Great Depression, but what had been the guesthouse, built in 1907 when Gamel was about eight and added to since then, remains the central family residence.

Sculpture Depicts America's "Assistant President"

Tucked away in a crook of the building near the main entrance is a diminutive statue that may not necessarily attract the attention of visitors to the Aiken County Courthouse. Yet this small bronze figure of a man in judicial robes is a monument to an Aiken resident who left his mark on the world's stage.

As the text carved on the plinth indicates, James F. Byrnes was "lawmaker, Supreme Court Justice, 'Assistant President,' Secretary of State, peacemaker, and Governor." Indeed, he is one of the very few individuals in our country's history that served in all three branches of the federal government.

Born in Charleston in 1882, Byrnes left school at the age of fourteen to help his mother take care of the family after the death of her husband. She is the one who taught him shorthand, and that skill helped Byrnes win a competition for the position of official court reporter or stenographer for the South Carolina Second Circuit. It was to take up his new duties that Byrnes moved to Aiken when he was only eighteen. During those early years, he taught himself the law and passed the bar examination.

Byrnes also dabbled in newspaper publishing. In fact, according to Donald M. Law's informal history of the *Aiken Standard*, Byrnes and his partner Alva Lorenz bought its precursor the *Aiken Journal and Review* in 1904 and expanded the circulation of that popular periodical. During what one might call his "newspaper years," he married Aikenite Maude Busch.

While still a resident of Aiken, Byrnes also set his sights on a political career. He ran for Congress as a Democrat and served as a United States representative from 1911 to 1925. When his time in Congress ended, so did his life in Aiken because he relocated his law practice to Spartanburg.

As the decade of the 1930s began, Byrnes himself started a ten-year tenure in the United States Senate until 1941, when he became a justice of the U.S. Supreme Court. One year later, at President Franklin Roosevelt's request, he resigned to become the director of the Office of Economic Stabilization and then the War Mobilization Board. Because of the power that he held over the nation's economy during those years, Byrnes was popularly known as the "Assistant President for the Home Front." Among his accomplishments in that office was the establishment of a budget for the Manhattan Project, which resulted in the development of the atomic bomb.

After the death of President Roosevelt, Byrnes served as secretary of state in the first two years of Harry Truman's presidency. This was probably the time of his greatest influence, and as chronicled in his book entitled *Speaking Frankly*, Byrnes was a key figure in shaping the peace of Europe; he attended seven international conferences and signed six treaties between 1945 and 1947. That same year, he gave his famous "Speech of Hope" in Stuttgart, Germany. In this address, Byrnes committed American troops to Europe as long as any other of the occupying powers, especially the Soviet Union, remained in Germany, and he gave the German people the hope that once again they might become prosperous and respected members of the world community.

After his resignation from the Truman cabinet in 1947, James F. Byrnes returned to South Carolina, where he was elected governor, an office he held from 1951 to 1955. His biggest achievement during his tenure in the state's highest office was to increase government support for public education. In 1953, for example, when the state government had a funding surplus, Byrnes dedicated all of the extra money to South Carolina's public-supported colleges. He died in 1972 in Columbia, where he is buried in the cemetery of Trinity Episcopal Church, just across the street from the statehouse.

Appropriately enough, it is on the corner of the statehouse grounds that faces his final resting place that a larger version of the Byrnes monument stands. Both the Aiken and Columbia statues were sculpted by Charles

The James F. Byrnes Monument. *Tom Mack.*

Parks. Based in Wilmington, Delaware, Parks has established a considerable reputation as an artist in the figurative tradition. Among his over five hundred sculptural works are five pieces in the permanent collection of Brookgreen Gardens near Myrtle Beach. His most famous work, however, is probably the nine-foot-tall sculpture entitled *Boy with Hawk*, which graces the entrance to the Brandywine River Museum, the world's most significant repository of works by N.C. Wyeth, Andrew Wyeth and other members of that distinguished family of artists.

Parks depicts Byrnes at the height of his powers in the decade of the 1940s—Byrnes was the *Time* magazine "Man of the Year" in 1946. Garbed in judicial robes, he sits on a bench whose four corners are adorned with Ionic volutes; both of his hands are folded over a book. A thoughtful, farsighted individual, Byrnes holds his head upright as if gazing confidently into the future.

Even a quick glance at his biography will lead one to the conclusion that James F. Byrnes lived the American dream, since he rose from humble origins to a position of power and fame. Yet his personal goals were never selfish; in fact, he once said, "My hope is that my experiences may encourage others to dedicate their talents and energies to public service for I believe with [Leo] Tolstoy that the 'sole meaning of life is to serve humanity.'" For area residents, it should be a matter of pride that in Aiken James Byrnes began charting his life's path.

COURTHOUSE MURAL SPARKS CONTROVERSY

When he created his New Deal in the 1930s, President Franklin D. Roosevelt envisioned a redistribution of our country's economic resources to benefit a broader spectrum of the population than had previously shared in our national bounty. Among those to whom the government would lend a helping hand were the artists, and major federal programs were created to support this group, who were suffering as much as the general population during the Great Depression.

Two of the most important New Deal programs established to put artists back to work were the Farm Security Administration's efforts to chronicle the plight of those who lived on the land—photographers such as Dorothea Lange, who recorded the lives of sharecroppers in South Carolina in 1936–37, created images that speak of one of the collective strengths of our people: a stubborn perseverance in the face of adversity—and the United States Treasury Department's Section of Fine Arts, which generally sponsored public art for public buildings.

One of the most significant works produced in South Carolina under the aegis of the latter program is the mural that was installed behind the judge's bench on the second floor of the Charles E. Simons Jr. Federal Courthouse on Park Avenue in Aiken.

The light brown curtain that hangs over the mural is a principal prop in one of the most interesting tales of art censorship in our country's history. Believe it or not, the 1938 installation of Stefan Hirsh's mural *Justice as Protector and Avenger* at the federal courthouse in Aiken created a whirlwind of criticism that cut a path from South Carolina to the District of Columbia. According to published records, local citizens accused the federal government of interference in their affairs by foisting on them the government-sponsored mural, and the presiding judge at the time felt that the wall painting distracted those in the courtroom from paying serious attention to official proceedings. The Treasury Department's Section of Fine Arts, on the other hand, accused local residents of both racial prejudice, since the central figure of Justice was termed by some local observers a "mulatto," and insensitivity to modern art, because some citizens were unable to appreciate the painting's mannered use of space, as well as its geometrically shaped human figures.

The mural itself, about twelve feet by twelve, is divided into three vertical panels. The central one is dominated by the imposing female personification of Justice, garbed in red, white and blue. With the clawlike fingers of her left hand, which she holds to her side in a protective posture, she indicates a sepia world of injustice, complete with arson and burglary. With her right hand, which is raised in a gesture of benediction, she reveals a world of law and justice, complete with agricultural bounty and family solidarity. It is a dramatic composition whose instant appeal makes one wonder what all the original fuss was about and why the mural remains covered to this day.

"My idea was to create a symbolic figure of 'Justice' with gestures indicating the meting out of justice to the deserving and the undeserving," commented the muralist about his own work. Born to American parents living in Germany, Hirsh enjoyed a distinguished career as an artist and art teacher. After his commissions for the Treasury Department's Section of Fine Arts, Hirsh went on to head the art department at Bard College in New York.

Now over seventy years after its installation, the final disposition of the Stefan Hirsh mural still needs to be resolved. My most recent perusal of the work, for example, was accomplished only after I made repeated phone calls to the office of the district judge. Surely a plan can

Stefan Hirsh's *Justice as Protector and Avenger. Lise Swensson and Nancy Higgins, New Deal Art in South Carolina, South Carolina State Museum.*

be developed that results in a better showcasing of one of Aiken's art treasures and one of the best-preserved government-supported murals produced during the Great Depression.

In 1990, when I first wrote about Hirsh's *Justice as Protector and Avenger*, I quoted the French painter Eugene Delacroix, who once wrote that "art is a clock that moves too fast when measured by the public sense of time." Perhaps, in the twenty-first century, we have reached a time when we can look at this matter with some perspective and resolve the issue in favor of art.

Those wishing more information on the mural's unhappy history may want to read the first chapter of Karal Marling's *Wall-to-Wall America* or the three pages devoted to the mural in the catalogue entitled *New Deal Art in South Carolina*, edited by Lise Swensson and Nancy Higgins.

Aiken

MEANING OF CAMPUS SCULPTURE DECODED

Visitors to the campus of the University of South Carolina–Aiken are often pleasantly surprised by the presence of the courtyard that graces the core of the Penland Administration Building, and they frequently pose questions about the origin and meaning of the bronze sculpture set in a special base in the center of that open-air space.

Fashioned by noted sculptor Charles O. Perry, *Double Knot* has come to symbolize, over time, the interlocking ties between the university and the community that it serves, but that was not necessarily the artist's original intention. As all good students know, much of the allure of great art lies in its susceptibility to multiple interpretations.

According to Perry himself, *Double Knot* is an exercise in topology, a branch of mathematics concerned with those properties of a geometrical configuration that remain unaltered even when twisted or stretched. In this regard, Sanford Wurmfeld, a member of the art faculty at Hunter College in New York, has argued that Perry's use of "certain mathematical concepts" makes it possible for him "to develop a vocabulary for the manipulation of forms in space." This manipulation, in turn, provides the viewer with a complex visual experience that changes as he or she moves around the sculpture, "at one moment seeing the combined whole of solid and void, at another, sensing the specific shapes of the metal forms, and yet another, revealing the independent form of the voids."

USCA's *Double Knot* stands in some very impressive company. Indeed there are Perry sculptures across the country in varied settings. *Continuum* stands in front of the National Air and Space Museum in Washington, D.C., and the thirteen-foot-tall, stainless steel sculpture entitled *Early Mace* is part of the fabric of the Peachtree Center in Atlanta. His most monumental work, however, is *Eclipse*, created in 1973 to adorn the seventeen-story atrium lobby of the Hyatt Regency Hotel in the four-block-long Embarcadero Center in San Francisco. This large-scale, perforated globe of brass-colored, anodized aluminum is balanced on four black pillars and further secured by a cable attached to one of the building's interior balconies. Obviously hotel officials are taking no chances should the giant thirty-five-foot orb begin to roll off its perch during one of the city's periodic seismic jolts!

Perry's work is also represented in the permanent collections of many important museums, including the Museum of Modern Art in New York, the Art Institute of Chicago and the San Francisco Museum of Art.

Charles O. Perry's *Double Knot. Tom Mack.*

The artistic legacy of Charles O. Perry has also been the subject of considerable attention at a number of notable venues. In 1998, some of his pieces were featured in a group exhibition at the National Academy of Design in New York City, and in 2000, he was honored by a one-person show at the Saint-Gaudens National Historic Site in Cornish, New Hampshire.

The latter show is particularly significant since both the Saint-Gaudens house and eighty-two-acre garden have been preserved in memory of Augustus Saint-Gaudens, the foremost American sculptor of the nineteenth century and a specialist in heroic civic monuments. Featuring Perry's work in a summer exhibition at this special spot places his work in the great tradition of American public sculpture.

Born in 1929 in Helena, Montana, Charles Owen Perry earned a master's degree in architecture from Yale University, and he worked as a professional architect in this country and in Italy while simultaneously experimenting with the art of sculpture. He organized his first one-man show of sculpture in San Francisco in 1964.

With the active intervention of Robert E. Penland, past chair of the Aiken County Commission for Higher Education, the sculpture *Double Knot* was donated to the university in honor of Perry's parents, Owen Hindmarch Perry and Margaret Carroll (Bache) Perry, in 1974. William Casper, USCA chancellor from 1963 to 1983, used to speak of the day that Charles Perry and his father Owen walked into his office in what then served as a general purpose classroom and office building for the whole campus. Perry's father Owen, who was a friend of Casper's in the Aiken Rotary, was justifiably proud of his son's work and eager to support USCA, which had just moved to its new campus. It was William Casper's ultimate decision to sanction the placement of the sculpture in the center of the courtyard of the administration building and to have it displayed on a pedestal surrounded by a circular bench.

A resident of Connecticut since 1977, Charles Perry is also noted for his chair designs, successfully marketed by such companies as Krueger International, Virco and Steelcase. He has also designed intriguing metal puzzles showcased at the Museum of Modern Art in New York and the Smithsonian in Washington.

It is truly a major artistic coup that USCA should possess an important work by a master of modern design.

PART II

Augusta

EIGHTEENTH-CENTURY NATURALIST
EXPLORED CSRA

"The village of Augusta is situated on a rich and fertile plain, in the Savannah River," wrote William Bartram regarding visits he made to the area in both 1773 and 1776. "[T]he buildings are near its banks and extend nearly two miles up to the cataracts, or falls, which are formed by the first chain of rocky hills, through which this famous river forces itself." Our country's first native-born naturalist, Bartram published his *Travels* in 1791; this landmark volume contains one of the earliest detailed descriptions of the Central Savannah River Area.

The son of John Bartram, who was appointed Botanist Royal in America by George III, William accompanied his father on an expedition to explore Florida in 1765–66 just after Britain had acquired the colony from Spain. Later, in 1773, when he was thirty-five, William Bartram set out on his own from his native Pennsylvania to explore the Southeast and record what he saw of the people, plants and animals of that region of what was soon to become a new nation.

In the spring of 1773, William Bartram landed in Savannah, and from that city, he set out for Augusta on the first of May with one companion, crossing from the Georgia side to the Carolina side of the river and back again. His principal intention was to attend an important Indian congress to be held in

Augusta. During this meeting, the Cherokees gave up a large tract of land, an estimated two million acres, in exchange for the cancellation of debts that they owed to European-American traders. As a consequence of this treaty, Bartram was able to join an eighty-member expedition organized in June to survey the newly acquired territory to the northwest of Augusta. His traveling companions were a very eclectic bunch, which included, according to Bartram, "surveyors, astronomers, artisans, chain-carriers, markers, guides, and hunters, besides a very respectable number of gentlemen, who joined us in order to speculate in the lands."

Much of the original Cherokee footpath that the group traversed to reach a spot called Cherokee Corners can be retraced today on secondary roads via car by using a map published in 2005 by the Classic South Regional Travel Association. The tour begins at exit 175 on Interstate 20 just north of Thomson and winds through Wrightsboro (originally a Quaker settlement), Crawfordville, Philomath and Lexington before ending about nine miles southeast of present-day Athens, Georgia.

Because of its central location and its stature as a center for trade between European settlers and Native Americans, Augusta served as the nexus of a number of Bartram's explorations of Georgia and South Carolina. He returned to the area, for example, in 1775 in order to explore more of what he called "Cherokee Country" in the mountains of North and South Carolina.

Two hundred years after Bartram's travels, a group from Augusta initiated a campaign to mark his route through the area; some parts of what is now called the Bartram Trail are covered by the Clark Hill Reservoir, but many sections can still be traced and some of the local Indian mounds that Bartram described along the way can still be seen.

The best source of information about Bartram's remarkable explorations is, of course, his own *Travels*, still in print in a variety of editions. The 1958 "naturalist's edition" annotated by Francis Harper is perhaps the most noteworthy. In addition, some dramatic excerpts from this groundbreaking work are often anthologized in American literature texts read by college students across the country.

In the first half of the sophomore survey of American literature, for example, I have often assigned my students to read Bartram's exciting account of his imperilment by alligators while navigating a "lake-like expansion" of the St. John's River in Florida. He wrote of how he was kept awake most of the night by the "loud and terrible roar" of hundreds of alligators who surrounded his camp; during this uneasy period, he was compelled to shoot

The Bartram Trail marker, Riverwalk, Augusta. *Michael Budd.*

some of the more venturesome intruders and club others on the head. So horrific was his experience with these Florida "monsters" that Bartram, according to one of his biographers, was plagued for years by nightmares.

Bartram's descriptive powers made his *Travels* one of the most influential books of his age. Scientists, as one would expect, were drawn to the book. In 1832, for example, naturalist and artist John J. Audubon, most famous for his monumental *Birds of America*, tried to witness for himself many of Bartram's discoveries. In 1845, British geologist Sir Charles Lyell used one of Bartram's references regarding fossilized tree stumps as partial proof of his principle of uniformitarianism, a concept that influenced the development of Charles Darwin's theory of evolution.

Interestingly enough, Bartram's description of the exotic regions that he explored also sparked imaginative responses from some of the leading European poets and novelists of the day. Scholars have already traced echoes of Bartram's imagery in *The Rime of the Ancient Mariner* and "Kubla Khan" by Samuel Taylor Coleridge and "The Prelude" and "The Excursion" by William Wordsworth. French novelist Chateaubriand's romantic conception of Native American life was inspired, in part, by Bartram's description of his dealings with the native people of North America.

It should, therefore, be a matter of some pride to local residents that one of the most influential early American writers crisscrossed this neck of the woods in pursuit of knowledge and that his written record of his scientific investigations should cast light on the flora, fauna and history of the Central Savannah River Area.

AUGUSTA PRESERVES TANGIBLE CONNECTIONS TO TWO SIGNERS

Essentially a four-sided block of stone carved into a tapering shape that has for its apex a pyramid, the obelisk was originally designed by the ancient Egyptians as a symbol of the sun ray. Over the centuries, because of its association with the symbolism of light as penetrating spirit, the obelisk has often been used for memorial purposes. The most famous American application of the obelisk shape, for example, is the Washington Monument, a white marble monolith completed in 1884 in Washington, D.C., to commemorate the life and work of our first president.

In Augusta is located another memorial obelisk. Although at fifty feet in height it is less than one-tenth the size of the Washington Monument, the Signers Monument in Augusta has a purpose just as grand as that of the giant obelisk in our nation's capital.

Buried in crypts beneath the marble obelisk on Greene Street are two of Georgia's three signers of the Declaration of Independence. Erected in 1848, the Signers Monument marks the graves of both Lyman Hall and George Walton. The final resting place of the state's third signer, Button Gwinnett, is still a matter of conjecture.

Born in Connecticut, Lyman Hall practiced medicine in South Carolina before acquiring plantations in Georgia along the Savannah River. Because of his early advocacy of the Revolution, Hall joined his friend Gwinnett in Philadelphia in 1776 as both served as members of Georgia's small delegation to the Continental Congress. Although there is no record of either man's taking an active part in the debates over independence, both Hall and Gwinnett are said to have been energetic committee workers, actively engaged in the managerial affairs of the Congress.

After Button Gwinnett's untimely death in 1777 in a duel with a political rival, Hall became his friend's executor before he himself was forced to

The Signers Monument. *Michael Budd.*

flee the state after the British captured Savannah. Both of his homes were burned, and some historians believe that Hall may have sought refuge with Connecticut relatives until the end of the war.

By 1783, Hall was back in Georgia, and he served for a time as governor of the state. He has been given credit for his advocacy of public higher education and agricultural reform. In 1790, Lyman Hall died on his plantation in Burke County, some twenty-five miles south of Augusta, and his body was moved to Greene Street in 1848 to rest beside that of George Walton.

At age twenty-six, Walton was one of the youngest signers of the Declaration of Independence. A native of Virginia, he moved to Savannah to study law in 1769. It was in Savannah that he helped organize two revolutionary conventions at the Tondee Tavern in 1774; both meetings elicited a largely apathetic response because of the colony's persistent loyalty to the Crown. Founded in 1733, Georgia was a relatively new colony and one that was still sparsely populated.

Despite its early inaction in the cause of liberty, Georgia made up for lost time in 1775 and 1776 by sending official delegates to the Continental Congress. Walton himself arrived in Philadelphia only days before July 4, just in time to sign the document.

Unlike Hall and Gwinnett, however, Walton lived long enough to make a substantial contribution to the life of his state. He survived the war despite being captured by the British at the siege of Savannah; as a colonel in the Georgia militia, he was traded for a high-ranking British naval officer. During the battle he was wounded in the thigh, and it is said that forever after he walked with a slight limp.

George Walton had a significant and varied career as a public servant. In addition to his work in Congress, he was twice elected governor of Georgia, and he also served as a Superior Court judge and chief justice of Georgia. Unlike Hall and Gwinnett, Walton called Augusta his home. According to some accounts, he was instrumental in revising the layout of the town, which for a time served as the state capital. Walton moved to a plantation he called Meadow Garden in 1790, and it was there that he died at the age of sixty-four in 1804.

The home, located near the corner of Thirteenth Street and Walton Way in Augusta, has long been a public museum administered by the Daughters of the American Revolution (DAR). Once situated on a tract of land of more than 120 acres, Meadow Garden is now surrounded only by a small plot bordered on one side by the Augusta Canal and on the other by modern industrial and commercial buildings.

The present structure has two floors, each with four rooms and a central hallway. It is evident from the asymmetrical front porch, however, that the home was built in two stages, for there are two sets of steps and two front doors, both on different levels. George Walton and his family most certainly resided in the half of the present structure nearest the canal.

Meadow Garden. *Tom Mack.*

Today the house includes fine examples of period furniture, including gold-trimmed china that may have belonged to the Walton family. The two basement rooms have been set up as a kitchen and workroom, and there is a replicated colonial garden on the grounds. For more information, visit Meadow Garden on the web at www.historicmeadowgarden.org.

WOODROW WILSON BOYHOOD HOME OFFERS MODEL OF RESTORATION

Since its official opening in 2001 following a ten-year, multimillion-dollar restoration, the boyhood home of the twenty-eighth president of the United States has become one of the most popular historic sites in Augusta. On average, three thousand visitors tour the house annually.

Located at the corner of Telfair and Seventh Streets, the boyhood home of President Woodrow Wilson takes the visitor back to the decade from 1860 to 1870, the period when the red brick, Greek Revival building first served as the manse for the First Presbyterian Church. As such, it was the comfortable residence of the Reverend Joseph Ruggles Wilson and his family during the years of the Civil War and early Reconstruction.

The house is situated just three blocks from Broad Street, and young Thomas Woodrow Wilson watched military parades march down Broad's wide expanse in the early years of the war; the house is also located just two blocks from an erstwhile railroad siding from which wounded troops disembarked for medical care at the First Presbyterian Church, whose pews had been removed to make way for hospital beds.

It has been conjectured that Wilson's early experience of the human cost of war contributed to his later ardent support of peacemaking efforts, especially his advocacy of the League of Nations.

His prominent role in world affairs, however, was still many years in the future when he lived in Augusta in the house now devoted to his memory. Today's visitors can obtain a guided tour of all three floors of this meticulously restored mansion.

The first floor, composed of four large rooms, two on each side of a long central hallway, boasts ceilings that are twelve feet high and walls painted their original colors, thanks to careful paint analysis. The two rooms to the

Woodrow Wilson's boyhood home. *Tom Mack.*

right of the hallway are the parlor and dining room, separated by their original pocket doors. Each features original furniture from the time of the Wilson family residency, including the dining table and marble-topped sideboard featuring carved game, a bird and a fish.

Thanks to the foresight of the congregation of the First Presbyterian Church, much of the house furniture was preserved, even after the church sold the manse in 1930. As a consequence, when Historic Augusta purchased the property in 1991 and began its painstaking refurbishment, there were in local hands many items once used by the Wilson family, furnishings carefully stored so that they could one day take their rightful place in their original setting.

Among the gems of the collection is a secretary used by the Reverend Wilson. The small bookcase on top has doors whose glass panels are silhouetted in a Moorish design. This desk is the centerpiece of the study to the left and rear of the first-floor hallway. It was here that Joseph Wilson read to his children, his son Tommy and his two daughters Marion and Annie (a fourth child, Joseph Jr., was born in the house in 1867), and it was here that Tommy Wilson's early lessons began under the supervision of his father.

History records that although he had a keen mind, the young Woodrow Wilson was somewhat indifferent to formal study. What captured his boyhood imagination most was baseball. In fact, on loose pages inserted into his geography book were found his handwritten constitution and bylaws for the Light Foot Baseball Club, a sports organization made up of neighborhood boys who met in the hayloft above the family carriage house, a structure still intact at the rear of the property.

The home's second floor is composed of five rooms, including three bedrooms, a dressing room and an informal family room. The third-floor attic is now devoted to a display area for photographs chronicling the building's admirably researched restoration.

The final result of the ten-year restoration project is a house museum that in my opinion rivals the finest examples of its kind in Charleston and Savannah in historical accuracy and skilled craftsmanship. The members of Historic Augusta are to be applauded for the diligence and sensitivity of their efforts to preserve a site so important to the history of our region and country.

Furthermore, this very active organization supervised the basic restoration of another significant historic structure, a building just next door to the Wilson Boyhood Home. This is the Lamar House, the former residence of Wilson's childhood friend and Light Foot Baseball Club teammate Joseph

Rucker Lamar, who served as a justice of the United States Supreme Court from 1910 to his death in 1916. The Lamar House is now used as a facility for meetings and receptions; it also contains a small gift shop.

For additional information on the Boyhood Home of President Woodrow Wilson, visit Historic Augusta on the web at www.historicaugusta.org.

AUGUSTA BREATHES NEW LIFE INTO OLD CANAL

When he visited Augusta in 1791, George Washington was already an advocate of water transportation. In fact, according to historian Edward Cashin, our first president had a dream that the United States would be linked one day by a commercial network of rivers and canals.

When Augusta finally constructed its canal in 1845, however, it was not transportation the city had in mind. It was power. Augusta wanted to harness water power for heavy industry, much as Lowell, Massachusetts, had done a few decades earlier. One cannot overestimate the significance of that momentous decision since most scholars ascribe the beginning of the industrial revolution in America to the development of the water-powered looms in Lowell's cotton mills.

Today, the Lowell canals are a major tourist attraction, but until fairly recently, the Augusta Canal was still being used largely for its original purposes: to generate power and provide drinking water. While this fact in itself affords the man-made waterway a unique place in our country's history, the recreational potential of this local community asset had gone largely unrecognized until the 1980s. Only then, with the advice of Boston-based consultants who had been instrumental in rehabilitating the Lowell canals, did Augusta residents start a campaign to restore their engineered waterway.

The redevelopment momentum accelerated when the United State Congress created the Augusta Canal National Heritage Area in 1996. Now, in addition to the eight and a half miles of towpath and waterway that have been preserved, there are ongoing plans to revitalize many of the landmarks along the path of the canal and fully restore downtown sections of the canal that had been filled in.

One of the Augusta landmarks to experience a new life is the once derelict Enterprise Mill. Long a feature of the city skyline because of its pair of

Enterprise Mill. *Michael Budd.*

ornate cupolas topped by wrought-iron weather vanes and lightning rods, the mill, built in 1877, was the target of a $17 million renovation in 1997 to convert much of the 260,000-square-foot property into loft apartments and office and commercial space.

A key part of the mill's refurbishment has been the establishment of the Augusta Canal Interpretive Center, which uses innovative multimedia exhibits to tell the story not only of the history of the canal but also of Augusta and the region. Any visit to the new center should begin with a stop in the theatre near the front entrance to view the informative short film on the making of the canal and its subsequent history.

Highlights of that history include the years of the Civil War when Augusta was the site of the Confederate States Powder Works, a complex of twenty-eight buildings running for two miles on both sides of the canal. In this enormous complex the Confederacy manufactured cannons, cartridges, grenades and signal rockets, as well as gunpowder.

Of equal significance in Augusta's history is the period immediately after the Civil War when the canal was greatly expanded, partially through the importation of Chinese labor, and the last two decades of the nineteenth century when a manufacturing boom caused the city to double in size and become an industrial center of the New South.

Progress, however, seldom comes without a price. The Augusta Canal Interpretive Center devotes attention to the regulated and restricted lives of the millworkers themselves—there is a partial re-creation of a company house, like those that still stand in Augusta and the Horse Creek Valley—and the attendant issues of child labor and unionization.

Available at the Interpretive Center is a free map that provides directions for a self-guided tour of the full length of the canal. From the Enterprise Mill, it is possible to walk or bike on the towpath or paddle a canoe up the canal all the way to the head gates in Columbia County. The Lockkeepers Cottage, in fact, is now the Savannah Rapids Regional Visitor Information Center, and restoration continues on the head gate and lock that will allow boat passage from the canal to the Savannah River.

From the dock at the Enterprise Mill, visitors can also take tours of the canal on a replica cargo vessel, called a Petersburg boat. Excursion tickets can be purchased at the Canal Interpretive Center; for more information, visit the canal on the web at www.augustacanal.com.

CONTROVERSIAL NOVELS STRADDLE BOTH SIDES OF RIVER

In his very influential 1953 study entitled *The Mirror and the Lamp*, M.H. Abrams identifies two contrasting metaphors for the imaginative process. According to Abrams, the work of a creative artist can be regarded either as a reflection of the world around him (the mirror) or as an outward projection of his own internal vision (the lamp).

The novels of Erskine Cardwell, particularly the abidingly controversial *Tobacco Road* and *God's Little Acre*, may very well exemplify both interpretations of the role of the artist and his work. Often hailed as a social realist with an uncanny ear for the dialect of the rural poor in his native Georgia, Caldwell frequently saw himself as holding up a mirror to the lives of ordinary people around him. Yet, as critics have pointed out, the author's views on politics and sex also find their way into his fiction, thus offering plenty of evidence that Caldwell's work was a vehicle of self-expression.

His most famous novel, *Tobacco Road*, is set in Georgia—Caldwell grew up near Wrens and worked for a time as a sports reporter for the *Augusta Chronicle*. On the south side of Augusta, there still exists a thoroughfare named Tobacco Road, now a five-lane highway that runs from Bush Field to Fort Gordon.

In Caldwell's novel, the road was a fifteen-mile, packed-dirt byway rambling along the ridges of the sand hills on the Georgia side of the Savannah River. Scattered along this pothole-marked trail were the homesteads of impoverished tenant farmers represented in the novel by the Lester family. The patriarch of the clan, Jeeter, refuses to abandon the farm, which had long ago been sold to others and which could no longer sustain even a subsistence living. He has an almost primordial attachment to tilling the soil, summed up in the statement of his son-in-law, Lov: "The ground sort of looks out after the people who keep their feet on it."

Despite his faith in plowing and planting—"it's in the blood"—his family is slowly starving. Most of his seventeen children either died young or ran away; all that remain in the ramshackle house are his wife Ada, suffering from pellagra and an addiction to snuff; his mother, who ingests boiled "leaves and roots" because her relatives have stopped sharing food with her; Ellie May, who still lives with her parents because men are repelled by her harelip; and sixteen-year-old Dude, whose unmindful youth serves as a talisman against despair. The ultimate fate of this illiterate, misguided and rapaciously self-serving bunch is, in turn, both comic and tragic.

Caldwell's second most significant book, *God's Little Acre*, takes place on both sides of the Savannah River; one-half of the novel is set on a farm on the Georgia side somewhere south of Augusta and the other half in the mill towns of the Horse Creek Valley between North Augusta and Aiken.

The title of the novel refers to Ty Ty Walden's promise to set aside an acre of his farmland to benefit the local church, but his fifteen-year quest to find gold on his property leads him to move the acre in question every time he decides on a new place to dig. In fact, he digs much more than he plants. As the novel begins, Ty Ty's obsession has so overruled his common sense that his family faces starvation.

His children can be defined in relationship to their father's gold fever. Two sons, Buck and Shaw, work on the farm. One son, Jim Leslie, has climbed his way up the social ladder to marry a girl from a good family and live in a fine old house in the section of Augusta still called "the Hill." One daughter, Darling Jill, still lives under her father's roof and according to her father's sense of individual license, but the other, Rosamund, resides across the river in South Carolina with her millworker husband, Will Thompson.

The character of Will Thompson affords Caldwell the opportunity to explore the employment conditions faced by most working-class southerners just before and during the years of the Great Depression. It was either the farm or the factory. Thompson calls Buck and Shaw, who labor for their father, "clodhoppers" and slaves of the soil; they, in turn, look down on their "lint-head" brother-in-law for his ministrations to the machine.

Yet it can be argued that Will Thompson is the hero of the book, for he is the leader of a group of men on strike for higher wages. His vow to turn the power back on at the mill closed by its owners energizes the citizens of Scottsville, a fictitious town that Caldwell adds to the string of mill villages on the real map between Aiken and Augusta: "Graniteville, Warrenville, Langley, Bath, and Clearwater."

The novel offers plenty of evidence of Caldwell's skill in replicating in words the natural and human topography of the Horse Creek Valley, from the man-made water resources to the ivy-covered mill buildings and the rows of identical company houses. Anyone who regularly drives from Aiken to Augusta, for example, can easily relate to the author's description of the trajectory of that journey: "When they got to the top of Schultz Hill, they could look down and see the muddy Savannah," the Fifth Street Bridge "and, on the Georgia side, the wide floodplain on which Augusta was built."

Published in 1933 but reprinted countless times since then and even made into a motion picture in 1958, *God's Little Acre* has often been the target of censorship. Even today some readers may find the book offensive in part because of Caldwell's depiction of the sexual mores of his characters. In this regard, it is difficult to say whether the men and women in the novel behave the way they do because Caldwell honestly believed that he was describing life as it is lived on the farms and in the factories of the South or because he intended them to act out his own personal philosophy that people are not fully themselves unless they follow their feelings.

Was he holding up a mirror or a lamp? You can be the judge. Since his death in 1987, Caldwell has been the subject of continuing critical interest. The University of Georgia Press has reissued nearly a dozen of his works in the last twenty years. Of particular note is the collaboration between Caldwell and photographer Margaret Bourke-White, his second wife, who set out from South Carolina to Arkansas to depict the plight of farmers in the American South during the Great Depression—the real-life counterparts of the characters depicted in his two landmark novels. Their 1937 collaboration entitled *You Have Seen Their Faces* is well worth a look.

Frank Yerby House
Gets Second Chance

History certainly can repeat itself. The proof of this assertion may be found, ironically enough, in the frequent fate of historic homes. These erstwhile residences are often provided a second chance to serve a useful purpose.

In 1987, for example, the Pickens-Salley House, the one-time home of two distinguished families, was moved in three parts from Kalmia Hill to the campus of the University of South Carolina–Aiken, where it now provides office space for certain key administrative functions.

In April 2008, a neglected literary landmark that once stood abandoned on the 1100 block of Eighth Street in downtown Augusta was reopened in its new setting on the campus of Paine College. It is the boyhood home of popular novelist Frank Yerby.

Thanks to the generosity of Allan Collier, the owner of a local firm that specializes in the construction of housing in the inner city, the Frank Yerby House was donated to Paine College in 2004 and moved to its present location on the corner of Laney-Walker Boulevard and Druid Park Avenue. Unlike the Pickens-Salley House, which survived its move more or less intact, the Yerby House suffered significant structural damage during and after its relocation. Nevertheless, some key elements of the building, such as the fluted staircase, flooring and bricks, were eventually incorporated into what has been described by college authorities as an accurate replica of the old house.

"Frank Yerby represents excellence," asserts Dr. George Bradley, president of Paine College, and that sentiment is echoed by countless readers. Yerby was a name that once reverberated on the bestseller lists. Starting in 1946 with the publication of his first novel *The Foxes of Harrow*, Frank Yerby wrote a total of thirty-three books that sold more than fifty-five million copies during his lifetime.

A historical novelist who blended accuracy of research with a compelling story line, Yerby produced works that soon attracted the notice of Hollywood. Set in New Orleans plantation society in the early 1800s, *The Foxes of Harrow* was made in 1947 into a film starring Rex Harrison and Maureen O'Hara. *The Golden Hawk*, which takes place in the West Indies in the seventeenth century, was translated for the screen in 1952; the movie featured Rhonda Fleming and Sterling Hayden. Ricardo Montalban starred in *The Saracen Blade*, a 1954 adaptation of a Yerby novel, which re-creates the culture of medieval Italy.

The Frank Yerby House. *Michael Budd.*

So adept was he at inhabiting characters from many countries and time periods that many readers had no clue that Yerby himself was African American. His father, Rufus Garvin Yerby, was a hotel doorman who had to travel to find work, leaving his mother Wilhelmina as the principal force in the lives of their children. Despite the humble circumstance of his birth, Yerby was fortunate enough to come from a family that valued schooling, and he pursued his primary and secondary education at the Haines Institute, a private school for black children in Augusta. He then went on to earn a BA in English from Paine College in 1937—during his time at Paine, he is credited with having written the school's alma mater—and an MA in English from Fisk University in 1938.

With the success of his first few novels, Yerby eventually made enough money to be able to live anywhere he wanted in the world, and he chose Spain. He moved to that country in the early 1950s and spent the last forty years of his productive life in that adopted land. Yerby died in Madrid in 1991.

Because of the breadth of his subject matter, only recently have scholars begun to reappraise Yerby's work in the context of the African American literary tradition. In this regard, his two novels *The Dahomean* and *A Darkness at Ingraham's Crest* have garnered the most serious critical attention since his death.

Taken together, these two books trace the fictional life of Nyasanu, the son of a chieftain in nineteenth-century Dahomey. In the first novel, the valiant Nyasanu faces a series of challenges to his young adulthood, including betrayal by his half-brother and his capture by a rival African tribe that sells him into slavery. The second novel picks up the narrative after Nyasanu, now renamed Wesley Parks, is transported to the American South.

Given Yerby's important place in the popular literature of the twentieth century, it is fitting that Paine College celebrates its ties to one of its most famous graduates by replicating the place where he spent his formative years. As a landmark of American literature and African American heritage, the Frank Yerby House deserves commemoration.

In this regard, I am happy to claim a modest role not only in the reclamation of Yerby's childhood home but also the restoration of his place in local history. When I saw in its original location the once-stately, two-story house whose flaking paint and boarded windows spoke eloquently of years of abandonment, I devoted one of my weekly columns to the topic of the neglected literary landmark and Yerby's largely forgotten roots in Augusta. In part because of the publicity provided by that column, which reached the hands of a number of influential people in the Central Savannah River Area, plans were generated to give the house a second life, and Paine College seized the opportunity to renew its ties to one of its most illustrious graduates.

For additional information on the Yerby House, visit Paine College on the web at www.paine.edu.

PART III

Edgefield

WILLOWBROOK CEMETERY
DESERVES RESTORATION

I have a confession to make: I like cemeteries, especially old ones. They can serve not only as peaceful settings for personal contemplation but also as significant registers of history.

In the latter regard, there is probably no regional burial ground more important than a little cemetery just two blocks from the town square in Edgefield. In fact, with the death of Senator Strom Thurmond in 2003, Willowbrook Cemetery was suddenly cast into the national spotlight.

The Thurmond plot is dominated by a large rectangular monolith framed by fluted pilasters and embellished with the official state seal of South Carolina. Interestingly enough, this particular monument was once a feature of the Thurmond plot in Bethany Cemetery at the top of Laurens Street in Aiken; it was undoubtedly the senator's original intention to be buried next to his first wife Jean Crouch, whom he married in the governor's mansion not long after his election as the state's chief executive in 1947. She died of cancer in 1960, and her remains were interred in Aiken in the large, otherwise empty plot still labeled "Thurmond" on its granite border.

The stone monolith, however, was moved from Aiken to Edgefield after his death; it now looms over the plot where his parents are buried. Directly under the shadow of that great upright block of stone is a flat marble slab covering

The Thurmond Memorial. *Tom Mack.*

the senator's grave. Carved on its rectangular surface is an impressive resume composed of over two dozen separate items, beginning with some recognition of his deep roots in the town and county of Edgefield, where he attended public school before graduating from Clemson University with a degree in horticulture. Thurmond worked as a farmer, teacher and coach before becoming county superintendent of schools from 1929 to 1933; he also read law with his father, passed the bar examination and served as city and county attorney from 1930 to 1938.

The stone grave covering also makes mention of two records he set while serving in the U.S. Congress, but one of those has been broken since his burial. Thurmond is still the "oldest person ever" to serve in the Senate—he was one hundred when he died—but the "longest serving member" is now Robert Byrd of West Virginia.

Strom Thurmond is but the latest in a long line of notable South Carolinians for whom Willowbrook has provided a final resting place. Just up a gentle ridge from the Thurmond family plot—the topography of Willowbrook is far from flat—is an older section crowded with nineteenth-century monuments, including grave markers commemorating the achievements of quite a few of our state's war heroes and public servants.

Among these is a square stone pillar with a Gothic Revival capital topped by the sculpture of a draped urn, a symbol of mourning. One of the inscriptions carved on this monument reads as follows: "Knightliest of the knightly race that since the days of old have kept the lamp of chivalry alight in hearts of gold." This elaborate memorial marks the burial place of Matthew Calbraith Butler, one of the most prominent cavalry officers of the Civil War and a prime example of one of the Old South's classic "cavaliers on horseback."

Very near the Butler monument in Willowbrook Cemetery is a blunt obelisk dedicated to the memory of another notable South Carolinian, Preston Smith Brooks. Famous not for his military prowess but for an act of

The Preston Brooks Monument. *Tom Mack.*

violence of a very different sort, Preston Brooks is often included in history books because of one deed that has come to symbolize the breakdown of our country's national debate over the issue of slavery.

In 1856, during a very emotional speech on whether Kansas should enter the Union as a free or slave state, Massachusetts senator Charles Sumner accused South Carolina senator Andrew Pickens Butler of luxuriating in a liaison with "the harlot, Slavery." Three days later, Brooks, a U.S. Congressman who was related to Senator Butler (who was, coincidentally, the uncle of Matthew Calbraith Butler) entered the Senate chamber after adjournment and attacked the unsuspecting

The grave site of Francis Pickens. *Michael Budd.*

Sumner, who was working at his desk, busily attaching his postal frank to his "Crime Against Kansas" speech. Sumner is said to have lurched blindly around the chamber while Brooks continued to beat him with a cane customarily used to discipline unruly dogs. Only after Sumner fell unconscious to the floor did Brooks withdraw from the chamber.

Both men became heroes to their respective constituencies. After a three-year period of recuperation, Sumner, a leading abolitionist, returned to Congress. After barely surviving a vote of censure, Brooks himself was reelected to his seat in the House of Representatives; he died of a respiratory infection in Washington in 1857 and was buried in Edgefield beneath a monument that reads, in part, that he exhibited "true patriotism" and that "the whole South unites with his bereaved family in deploring his untimely end."

On the same knoll crowned by both the Butler and Brooks monuments is the Pickens family plot, the final resting place of a couple whose public and personal history still resonate in both Edgefield and Aiken. Francis Pickens was governor of South Carolina at the outbreak of the Civil War; his third wife, Lucy Holcombe Pickens, was considered the quintessential southern belle. He died only a few years after his service as "war governor," but she lived on until 1899. The inscription on her flat stone grave covering reads: "[B]eautiful in person, cultivated in mind, patriotic in spirit, she was loved by all who knew her."

In 1986, the Pickens family home, known as Edgewood, was donated to the University of South Carolina–Aiken; it now serves to house administrative offices. Unfortunately, the Pickens plot has not fared as well as their historic Edgefield residence. Today the stucco is crumbling on the brick fence that surrounds the twelve family graves, and weeds have spread across the unraked gravel that serves as an interface for the memorials.

In fact, a general air of disrepair pervades the whole cemetery, which has been the object of more than one aborted attempt at restoration in recent years. Some serious attention to refurbishing this important historic site is long overdue.

ENSLAVED POTTER LEFT HIS MARK

Edgefield pottery is unique in ceramic history because of the glaze made from timber ash and lime. The vessels themselves are largely utilitarian in nature, articles to be used in the daily activities of agrarian plantation life. It is the

alkaline-based glaze—usually khaki in color—that makes the pottery distinctive; this coating was developed as an inexpensive, safe alternative to the once popular lead glaze found to be dangerous as early as the eighteenth century.

Modern interest in Edgefield pottery, however, can be traced largely to the 1919 acquisition by the Charleston Museum of a jar enigmatically signed "Dave." Research to discover the identity of this then unknown potter eventually led to an enhanced understanding of the entire alkaline-glazed stoneware tradition centered in the Old Edgefield District, which encompassed present-day Greenwood, Edgefield and Aiken Counties in South Carolina.

It is interesting to note, however, that ninety years of biographical investigation has resulted in the uncovering of very few facts about Dave's life beyond some basic information gleaned from a perusal of census records and property tax inventories.

It is now assumed that Dave was born about 1800, and much of the subsequent information that historians have been able to assemble has come from examining the records of the families that ran the principal pottery works in the region. Over time he was bought and sold by the Drake, Gibbs, Miles and Landrum families. Dave, for example, was the property of Harry Drake until the latter's death in 1832. After emancipation in the 1860s, Dave took the last name of Drake, perhaps in commemorative remembrance of the man who presumably taught him to be a potter.

There is some conjecture concerning why Dave never left the Edgefield District, even though some members of the Drake and Gibbs families moved west to Louisiana, taking some of Dave's relatives with them. Presumably Dave was too valuable a resource for his employers where he was. As a skilled potter, he had a place.

Despite the paucity of written records about Dave's whereabouts and welfare, the visual record offers some compelling, compensatory information. There are thirty years of verified work, from 1834 to 1864, and the jars and jugs produced during this period provide more than just Dave's signature and their date of production.

Size and text make the "Dave pots" the most important specimens of Edgefield pottery. Most of Dave's vessels are of a remarkable size, with capacities sometimes ranging from twenty-five to forty gallons. Dave must have been a man of great strength since it is theorized that he probably had to manipulate up to fifty pounds of clay while kicking a foot or treadle wheel. Each large piece was made by joining separately constructed sections. The base was turned on the wheel while the upper parts, the shoulder and mouth,

Food storage jar, David Drake, August 24, 1857. *McKissick Museum, University of South Carolina.*

were applied to the base in coils and then seamlessly attached by smoothing the clay together. The last step before firing was the application of a drippy, ash-based alkaline glaze. From the 1820s to the 1860s, Dave may have made more than forty thousand pieces, including countless examples of these mammoth vessels usually with slab or ear handles and rolled rims.

Besides their extraordinary size, Dave's pots are unusual for their inscribed texts. In 1840, Dave began signing his work, not by merely stamping his initials on the base, as was the custom, but by boldly writing "Dave" on the shoulder of most vessels. He is known to have signed and dated over one hundred jars, and on some he wrote verse. This was a remarkable gesture. At a time when the South forbade the education of slaves, Dave was publicly demonstrating his ability to read and write.

His self-assertion did not go without notice. There was, indeed, a seventeen-year period of poetic silence on Dave's part, and some scholars theorize that a suppressed slave uprising in Augusta, Georgia, in 1841 may have been the cause. Because of the discovery of a plan to raid the Augusta arsenal and burn the city, the slave population in the region suffered through a period of repression, and Dave may have thought it best not to call attention to himself for a time.

Much of Dave's verse reflects the conditions of his life. For example, the lines "I wonder where is all my relations/Friendship to all and every nation" may be, in part, a reference to the constant threat that slaves could be sold and separated from their families. Although he publicly lamented this practice, for instance, Governor Francis W. Pickens, the biggest slave owner in the Edgefield District, was known to sometimes break up families.

Another rhyming couplet, "the forth [sic] of July is surely come/to blow the fife and beat the drum," is perhaps a reference to the fact that slaves were prohibited from beating drums because the white population feared the African use of percussion instruments as communication devices, as the potential means of linking widely scattered plantation populations.

Some verses may have reflected Dave's personal strategies for survival. One of his most famous couplets, "Dave belongs to Mr. Miles/where the oven bakes and the pot biles [sic]," may be seen not only as an acknowledgment of his condition as someone's property but also as an assertion that he is a literate artisan and, therefore, a man of value, one worthy of sufficient sustenance. At this time in his life, Dave was owned by Lewis Miles and lived near Graniteville.

The passage of time has affirmed Dave's status as a master craftsman whose work is unique in the history of American ceramics. Indeed, the McKissick Museum at the University of South Carolina in Columbia mounted in 1998 a major exhibition devoted solely to his achievement. Entitled I Made This Jar, the show traveled to three other museums across the country; for more information, I recommend the informative catalogue written by Jill Beute Koverman.

OAKLEY PARK STANDS AS RED SHIRT SHRINE

"Hooray for Hampton! Hooray for Hampton!" shouted approximately 1,500 men as they marched through downtown Edgefield on their way to the courthouse to cast their ballots in the gubernatorial election of 1876. According to local lore, these men had come from all parts of the county to gather on the grounds of Oakley Park, the home of General Martin Witherspoon Gary, in preparation for this demonstration of their united support for candidate Wade Hampton III, a war hero and the scion of a distinguished line of antebellum planters.

At stake in the momentous state election of that year was the reestablishment of the old order in South Carolina, a return to home rule after over ten years of federal intervention following the Civil War. The followers of Hampton, noted for the red shirts they wore as emblems of allegiance to his leadership, developed an election strategy that, according to historian Walter Edgar, had the "precision" of a military campaign.

It is, therefore, not surprising that Edgefield native Martin W. Gary should have been at the forefront of those seeking Hampton's victory. After all, General Gary himself had battlefield experience with the Seventh South Carolina Cavalry; when General Robert E. Lee surrendered at Appomattox, the stunned Gary, according to Edgar, "cursed while his hardened veterans wept" in collective disbelief.

More than a decade later, however, General Gary's political strategizing met with a far happier fate than did his military efforts. Although the 1876 election results were contested by the Reconstruction-era Republicans then in control of state government, and though South Carolina was made to endure four months with two rival governors and two rival general assemblies, Hampton and his fellow Democrats eventually assumed control after President Rutherford B. Hayes withdrew federal troops from the state in April 1877.

Now touted as the only shrine to the Red Shirt Movement, Oakley Park, home of both General Gary and his nephew Governor John Gary Evans, is operated today as a public museum in Edgefield. Surrounded by seven acres of land, the house still boasts many of the features in place during General Gary's time.

There is still, for example, the narrow central balcony from which he is said to have rallied his men on that fateful election day in 1876. This occasion offered yet another opportunity for Gary to justify the appropriateness of his wartime nickname "the Bald Eagle," a sobriquet he earned in part for his piercing eyes and in part for his shrill voice that could be heard above a crowd.

Among other features dating from Gary's tenancy in the house are hand-carved moldings and mantels and seven pieces of the general's own furniture, including an elaborate hall tree in the first-floor entryway, a plantation desk, a rocking chair and an assortment of bedroom furnishings. Other notable

Oakley Park. *Tom Mack.*

pieces donated to the house are an original red shirt, dyed its characteristic color by the use of pokeberry juice, and a valuable corner china cabinet made by skilled slave labor.

Gary was only fifty when he died in the house, which was then inherited by his sister, who deeded it to her son John Gary Evans. One of the ten governors that called the Edgefield District their home, Evans lived in Oakley Park until his death in 1941—he is buried in Willowbrook Cemetery.

Edgefield

The house holds many mementos of his life and career. He practiced law in Aiken before devoting himself to politics, serving as South Carolina's youngest governor—he was only thirty-one when he was elected—and the one who presided over the writing of the current constitution in 1895. The subject of ongoing controversy, this is the document that confirmed the central role of the legislature in South Carolina at the expense of a relatively weak executive branch.

Built in 1835, Oakley Park is the object of continuous restoration by Chapter 1018 of the United Daughters of the Confederacy, the organization now responsible for its maintenance. According to Carolyn Piekielniak, curator and hostess, the group recently received a $150,000 state grant, making it possible to restore the front parlor, begin restoration on the back parlor/library, update the kitchen for catering purposes and solicit bids for the installation of central air and heating.

To cover the cost of preserving the home and its grounds, which also features a kitchen house dating from 1865, an admission fee is charged and donations are gratefully accepted. Oakley Park is located at 300 Columbia Road in downtown Edgefield.

GRAVES TELL STORIES OF TWO CAROLINAS

In Edgefield County are located two historic cemeteries that signal a pivotal moment in our state's history. Willowbrook in the town of Edgefield contains the grave of Matthew Calbraith Butler, a Civil War hero and descendant of an old southern family; Ebenezer Cemetery in Trenton boasts the gravesite of Benjamin Tillman, a fiery advocate of government reform. Their respective memorials bear witness to a political struggle that marked the moment that South Carolina shed its allegiance to the Old South and embraced some of the values of the New.

On Church Street in downtown Edgefield, in the upper reaches of a narrow rectangle of land whose varying elevation bears witness to the fact that it once formed the banks of a woodland brook, stands the memorial to Matthew Calbraith Butler. The fragment of verse carved on one side of this vertical column topped by a draped urn, a traditional symbol of mourning, reads as follows: "Knightliest of the knightly race that since the days of old have kept the lamp of chivalry alight in hearts of gold." This first stanza

The Matthew Calbraith Butler Monument. *Tom Mack.*

from the poem "Virginians of the Valley" by physician-poet Francis Orrery Ticknor of Columbus, Georgia, calls attention not only to Butler's celebrated career as a much-decorated cavalry officer in the Civil War but also to his elevated social status as a member of the planter class that controlled the state for generations.

Edgefield

Born in Greenville in 1836 but a resident in Edgefield beginning in 1851, Butler was the son-in-law of and campaign manager for Francis Pickens, whose election as governor in 1860 confirmed the secessionist inclinations of the political leadership of the state. When war came shortly thereafter, Butler, who was then in the state legislature, volunteered as a captain of cavalry and served gallantly in the Army of Northern Virginia from the First Battle of Manassas until the spring of 1865. He saw action in many significant engagements, and he was periodically cited for bravery and eventually promoted to major general. At the Battle of Brandy Station in 1863, Butler lost his right foot to a cannonball; his wife Maria Pickens Butler and her father, at that point no longer governor, journeyed to Richmond to attend to his medical needs. When he returned to service, Butler took part in many of the battles fought in defense of the Confederate capital, and he remained in Virginia until ordered home to South Carolina to help impede General Sherman's advance across the state.

Like so many members of his class, Butler faced financial ruin after the war; it is said, in this regard, that he advised his stepmother-in-law Lucy Pickens to rent out Edgewood, now the Pickens-Salley House on the campus of the University of South Carolina–Aiken, to avoid some of the high tax burden under which property owners labored during Reconstruction. Eventually, in 1876, Butler came to the support of his former commander, General Wade Hampton, in the latter's bid for the governorship. Hampton's election in 1876 signaled the end of federal military occupation of the state and the restoration of home rule. In essence, the elite minority that had controlled South Carolina before the Civil War was once again in power.

The primary concern of Wade Hampton and his supporters was to restore what had been lost. Walter Edgar asserts that "as former Confederate officers and scions of some of the state's oldest families, South Carolina Bourbons (for the French royalists who resumed power after Napoleon and acted as if nothing had changed) did not expect to be questioned or challenged." In general, they tended to resist new ideas in favor of holding on to the remnants and relics of the old order; in particular, they encouraged the sanctification of the Southern defeat in the war in what came to be called the cult of the Lost Cause.

All of this changed dramatically in 1890 with the election to the state governorship of yet another Edgefield County resident, the controversial Ben Tillman. His monument in Ebenezer Cemetery at the corner of East Wise Street and Airport Road in the small, well-tended community of Trenton prefigures the memorials to most modern politicians in that it rejects the

The Benjamin Tillman Monument. *Michael Budd.*

traditional funerary symbols in favor of plenty of blank space upon which to carve the dead person's extensive curriculum vitae.

In the case of Benjamin Ryan Tillman, a prosperous farmer from Edgefield County who entered state politics at the head of a group of men intent on agricultural reform, the first item on his impressive tombstone resume is the governorship of South Carolina. Tillman stunned the members of the Bourbon establishment, who had heretofore counted on their military service to keep them in office, by taking control of the Democratic Party in the state in 1890 and thus ensuring his election.

Often charged with political demagoguery, Tillman was adept at swaying a crowd by frequently appealing to their fears and prejudices. On both his grave marker in Trenton and the monument dedicated to him on the statehouse grounds in Columbia is carved the assertion that "loving them, he was the friend and leader of the common people." He served two terms as governor before setting his sights on the United States Senate seat then occupied by Matthew Calbraith Butler, who had been in Washington for eighteen years, ever since 1877 after he had helped Wade Hampton wrest control of the statehouse from Reconstruction Republicans. By the senatorial election of 1894, Butler knew that he didn't stand a chance against Tillman's political machine, but according to Walter Edgar, he put up a fight in what was to be a very bitter campaign. With Butler's ultimate defeat came the end of state control by Hampton and his allies.

With the ascendancy of "Pitchfork Ben" Tillman came the values of the New South, both good and bad. On the one hand, there was a greater emphasis on regional boosterism, entrepreneurial business practice and industrial arts education; with Tillman's solid support, Clemson Agricultural College was founded as a "practical" alternative to what was perceived as the elitist, liberal arts–centered values of South Carolina College, as the University of South Carolina was then called. On the other hand, Tillman encouraged the disenfranchising of African Americans and set the stage for twentieth-century racial segregation in South Carolina.

Butler died in Columbia in 1909. Tillman died while serving in the United States Senate in Washington in 1918, his twenty-third year in that office. Their graves in Edgefield County, roughly seven miles apart, symbolize two very different visions of South Carolina.

PART IV

And Beyond

SOUTH CAROLINA NATIVE
BECAME FIRST NATIONAL ARCHITECT

"We have entered a new era in the history of the world; it is our destiny to lead and not be led. Our vast country is before us and our motto, Excelsior," wrote Robert Mills, who is regarded by historians as the first American-born architect. He is also one of South Carolina's most distinguished native sons.

Born in Charleston in 1781, Robert Mills submitted his earliest professional drawings for a competition to design the principal building of South Carolina College, now the University of South Carolina in Columbia. Even though his plan was not chosen, Mills was encouraged by its general reception and his modest remuneration.

Although USC-Columbia regrettably lost its chance to boast possession of a building designed by Mills, our region is graced by a number of structures that bear the stamp of his genius, including the First Presbyterian Church on Telfair Street in Augusta and two landmarks in Columbia.

In 1820, Mills was appointed "Civil and Military Engineer of the State." His new responsibilities included the construction of what was then called the State Insane Asylum in Columbia. Into his plan Mills incorporated some of the more enlightened theories of his day, regarding the treatment of the mentally ill: private rooms, exercise space and a roof garden. Now registered as a national landmark, the Mills Building remained part of the architectural

The Robert Mills House. *National Park Service.*

fabric of the South Carolina State Hospital until recent efforts to downsize government led to a decision to place the property on the market.

A more accessible example of the architectural genius of Robert Mills is the house museum on Blanding Street. Known today at the Robert Mills House, this is one of the very few residential structures designed by Mills. Built between 1823 and 1825 for English merchant Ainsley Hall and his wife Sarah, who grew up outside of Columbia, the house was never inhabited by its intended owners due to Hall's untimely death; for most of its history it served as the centerpiece of a number of educational institutions until reclaimed by the Historic Columbia Foundation in 1967. Occupying an entire city block, the four-acre property boasts the main house and a very attractive formal garden with indigenous nineteenth-century plants growing in boxwood-framed beds crisscrossed by gravel walkways.

Mills's reputation as a perfectionist can still be seen in the house's extraordinary symmetry. The door to the enclosed staircase on one side of the curvilinear entrance hall, for example, is balanced on the other side by a fake door; all four beautifully proportioned formal rooms on the first floor feature tall windows with pocket shutters and intricately carved crown molding.

And Beyond

His success with public buildings eventually led Andrew Jackson to appoint Mills as federal architect, and he served seven presidents in that capacity. Perhaps his most notable accomplishment during that period was the design and construction of the Treasury Building; a splendid engraving of this structure is on the ten-dollar bill. Mills's designs are noted for the soundness of his engineering, his use of iron girders and thin, strong, fire-resistant, hydraulic cement vaulting. His achievement in construction is even more remarkable in light of the fact that he had no modern machinery at his disposal. The Fifteenth Street façade of the Treasury Building, for example, has thirty-four Ionic columns, each thirty-six feet high; all were lifted into place by a block and tackle method, using a team of sixteen oxen.

Despite his many designs for public buildings and private houses, however, Robert Mills's reputation today rests largely on his creation of memorials commemorating the American Revolution, including the Washington National Monument. Earlier than the construction of that iconic memorial, however, Mills designed for Baltimore this country's first monument to Washington; it is a stout Doric column crowned by an eighteen-foot statue of Washington by Italian sculptor Enrico Causici. The memorial was one of the few things the often-acerbic English novelist Charles Dickens praised about this country on his first American tour in 1842.

On a trip to Baltimore some years ago, I remember climbing the 228 steps that spiral to the top of the monument in order to get a bird's-eye view of the city. Located just ten blocks from Baltimore's rejuvenated Inner Harbor, the monument towers over the historic Mount Vernon neighborhood, which is also home to the Walters Art Gallery and the Peabody Conservatory of Music.

Four years after the construction of the Baltimore memorial, plans for a Washington Monument in our nation's capital city were initiated; the site was said to be one designated by Washington himself in 1783 for his own victory memorial. The original design by Robert Mills called for a circular, colonnaded building from which sprang a five-hundred-foot Egyptian-style obelisk. With the temple base, which was to contain Washington's tomb, left off the final construction, the monument was not completed until twenty-nine years after Mills's death in 1855 because of periodic controversy and funding shortfalls.

Today, it stands as a memorial not only to our nation's first president but also to our nation's first native-born professional architect, a native son of South Carolina.

REDCLIFFE PLANTATION RECALLS HEYDAY OF KING COTTON

Among the almost fifty properties managed by the South Carolina State Park Service are three historic mansions: Hampton Plantation about halfway between Charleston and Myrtle Beach; Rose Hill Plantation eight miles south of Union; and Redcliffe Plantation, right in Aiken County. The family seat of James Henry Hammond and three generations of his descendants, this impressive house, along with its grounds and outbuildings, provides ample evidence of how the wealthy planter class lived before and after the War Between the States.

In 1859, just two years after he delivered his now famous "Cotton is King" speech to the United States Senate, James Henry Hammond built his two-story mansion at Redcliffe, a four-hundred-acre property that he had purchased near Beech Island in 1855. This particular parcel of land was never meant to be a working plantation; Hammond already had several of those, including the three-thousand-acre Silver Bluff Plantation about seven miles away near present-day Jackson. The latter property he had acquired in 1831 through marriage to Catherine Elizabeth Fitzsimons, an heiress, then seventeen years old.

At Redcliffe, Hammond hoped to build a home worthy of his stature as a great landowner, notable politician (he served as a United States Representative in 1834–36, South Carolina governor in 1842–44 and United States Senator on the eve of the Civil War) and the founder of what he envisioned as a family dynasty.

Although he possessed many positive qualities, including intelligence, energy and strength of will, Hammond was also capable of being his own worst enemy. He saw women only in the light of their use; an attempted dalliance with one of his nieces caused a barely repressed scandal, and his sexual relationships with female slaves prompted a temporary separation from his wife. He was also an incorrigible bully; he often browbeat his two sons, and he even tried to dictate economic policies to the Confederate government in Richmond.

The war took a heavy toll on Hammond's health—he died in 1864—and on his property. In his journal, he railed against government appropriation of his crops and the impressing of his slaves, and he worried about the fate in combat of his progeny. All three of his sons, however, survived the war, and the eldest, Harry—who eventually rose to the rank of major and was among those who surrendered with Lee at Appomattox—inherited Redcliffe, named for the "red bluff in front of it."

And Beyond

Redcliffe. *Tom Mack.*

Even with the alterations and embellishments of succeeding generations, the house itself is remarkably unchanged from Hammond's day. The original interior plan is intact, with four large rooms on the two principal floors, each room opening to a large central hallway. The main rooms on the first floor boast fourteen-foot-high ceilings with original decorative moldings. The floorboards, too, are intact, and the doors and mantelpieces are original, all made from sycamore wood presumably harvested on the plantation. The building is, in short, a gem of historic preservation.

Much of the credit in this regard belongs to John Shaw Billings, the great-grandson of James Henry Hammond and, at one point, the editorial director of all Time, Inc. publications, including *Time*, *Life* and *Fortune* magazines. A millionaire from all of the stock that he owned in the company for which he worked, Billings bought Redcliffe in 1935 from his uncle Henry Hammond and set about preserving and restoring the estate, which he eventually willed to the State of South Carolina before his death in 1975.

It was Billings who converted two rooms, one on the first floor and one on the second, to a library for the family book collection, including travel volumes once owned by James Henry Hammond, who made more than one trip to Europe, where he purchased items for the house.

Restored slave quarters at Redcliffe Plantation State Park. *Michael Budd.*

Among those souvenirs of the grand tour is a painting that has been ascribed to the seventeenth-century French master Georges de la Tour. Influenced by the groundbreaking work of Michelangelo de Caravaggio, De la Tour experimented with the effects of dramatically contrasting light and dark. The work that Hammond purchased, however, has suffered from so much overpainting through the years that its authenticity may never be fully validated.

In his own version of the grand tour in 1855, Hammond's son Harry brought back the other most notable painted work preserved in the collection, a copy of Raphael's *The Transfiguration*. In the nineteenth century, it was common to pay for copies of the works of the so-called Great Masters, and any work by Raphael certainly qualified in this category. *The Transfiguration*, considered Raphael's last significant painting, probably finished by one of his students after his death in 1520, is a large-scale work. Measuring nearly seven feet wide and eight feet tall, the Hammond copy is around two-thirds of the size of the original, but like the original, the copy is divided into two parts; the bottom half features an exorcism of a demon-possessed boy by the twelve apostles, whose efforts prove fruitless until the risen Christ appears in the cloud-filled sky, bracketed by two Old Testament prophets, Moses and Elijah.

And Beyond

As with any historic site, Redcliffe is the subject of ongoing preservation and interpretation. Greater emphasis, for example is now being placed on the stories of the African American slaves who worked the property. Among the existing outbuildings are two former slave quarters, one subsequently converted by Billings into a garage. There were originally four such structures at Redcliffe, each housing two families. As modern historians have devoted more research to the lives and contributions of the enslaved population in antebellum society, these quarters have become the locus of more and more interest. The remaining duplex features back-to-back fireplaces; displayed on the interior walls are copies of vintage photographs of individuals who served the Hammond family over generations.

Access to the grounds is free, but there is a charge for tours of the house. For additional information, visit the South Carolina State Park Service on the web at www.southcarolinaparks.com.

HARLEM MUSEUM SHOWCASES LEGENDARY COMEDIANS

When the United States Postal Service decided in 1991 to commission a series of stamps to honor classic comedians, one famous duo topped the list of those to be commemorated: the British-born Stan Laurel and Georgia-bred Oliver Hardy. In one of the five commemorative stamps featuring the work of noted caricaturist Al Hirshfeld, the two partners are captured in a characteristic interaction. On the left side of the image, the thin, diminutive Laurel sports a wide, goofy grin, and on the right side, the rotund, mustachioed Hardy gives his partner an exasperated glare. One can almost hear Hardy utter his famous catchphrase, "This is another fine mess that you've got us in."

Over the course of three decades, from the late 1920s to the early 1940s, Laurel and Hardy made a score of popular films, both short and feature length, that made them international celebrities. In each of these screen narratives, the meek Laurel and the more assertive Hardy generally get entangled in some ill-conceived or poorly implemented scheme. In the 1933 film *Sons of the Desert*, "the boys," as they were affectionately called by fans, get caught trying to deceive their wives in order to attend a national convention of their fraternal organization; in the 1937 film *Way Out West*, the duo try to honor the wishes of a dying man by conveying the deed to a gold mine to his daughter and heir, but they end up giving the valuable document to the wrong person.

Despite their often stumbling, bumbling manner, Laurel and Hardy generally find a way to correct their mistakes and right the wrongs perpetrated by others. In perhaps my favorite of their films, the 1934 *Babes in Toyland*, for example, the boys, boarders at the home of the Widow Peep, help her daughter Bo marry her beloved Tom-Tom and, in the furtherance of their personal goals, coincidentally save their fanciful homeland from invading monsters.

This now legendary comic duo was established in 1927 at the studio of Hal Roach in Culver City, California, but they arrived at their momentous union from different routes. Born in Ulverston, England, in 1890, Stan Laurel led a largely itinerant childhood because his father was a professional performer in British music halls. Laurel came to America in 1910, touring in vaudeville until he found himself in the motion picture industry. Hardy was born in 1892 in Harlem, just to the west of Augusta, and he got his start in show business in Milledgeville when he took a job in 1910 as a projectionist and singer in a movie house called the Electric Theatre. Enamored of the films that he showcased, Hardy decided to follow his dream of appearing on the screen himself. He worked in motion picture studios in Jacksonville, Florida, and then in New Jersey before moving to California in 1919.

Until recently, Hardy's roots in Georgia were largely unacknowledged. In 2002, with the opening of the Laurel and Hardy Museum in Harlem, Ollie Hardy's early years have now come into sharper focus. Previously a construction crew foreman for the Georgia Southern Railroad, which was then building a rail line between Augusta and Madison, Hardy's father was, at the time of Oliver's birth, managing a hotel in Madison. Oliver Hardy was born in Harlem because his mother, Emily Norvell, was "confined" during her pregnancy to the home of her parents, who were residents of that town. Only ten months after Oliver was born, however, his father died suddenly of a heart attack and was buried in Harlem. The rest of the family then moved to Atlanta and eventually to Milledgeville, where his mother managed the Baldwin Hotel; it was in Georgia that Oliver discovered his talent for music (he had a fine singing voice) and comedy.

The Laurel and Hardy Museum in Harlem showcases lobby cards, posters and stills from the duo's films, innumerable examples of Laurel and Hardy–inspired merchandise and a host of fan tributes. Particularly interesting are items manufactured abroad, including Laurel and Hardy comic books printed in the Netherlands and Laurel and Hardy calendars from Italy and

The Laurel and Hardy Museum. *Tom Mack.*

Germany. There are also some props from Laurel and Hardy films, including a fez worn in *Sons of the Desert.*

The museum is located in downtown Harlem in a building that once housed the town's post office. Every fall, Harlem hosts an Oliver Hardy Festival, which features a parade, street dance and hundreds of crafters and vendors. For additional information, visit the museum on the web at www.laurelandhardymuseum.org.

PARK INTERPRETS SOUTH CAROLINA'S ONLY PRESERVED CIVIL WAR BATTLEFIELD

"If you are still in Aiken, leave at once." wrote Private Sydney Ashe Legare of the Third South Carolina Cavalry to his wife after the Battle of Rivers Bridge. "Sherman is advancing rapidly up along the river. If we cannot hold this line (and it looks like it), the road from Augusta to Branchville will be given up."

Unknown to him at the time, Legare had just taken part in the Confederacy's most significant resistance to the advance of Sherman's army on its march from Savannah, Georgia, through South Carolina. With the state's capital city, Columbia, as his primary target, Sherman had ordered an assault against the Confederate's main defensive line, a series of three bridges set at six-mile intervals along the Salkehatchie River.

The central bridge, known as Rivers Bridge, offered the greatest challenge to the Union forces since contemporary accounts describe the Salkehatchie at that point as more swamp than river. Yet, on February 2, 1865, the First Division of the Seventeenth Corps under the command of General Mower, nicknamed "the Swamp Lizard," waded through "icy water that was often waist deep" to make a frontal assault on the Confederate breastworks on the north side of the river. The Confederate forces, under the command of General McLaws, were nevertheless easily able to repulse the attack due to the advantage of their skillfully placed earthworks that provided them with cover while they focused "their fire on the plank causeway that led to the bridge."

The Union assault on February 2 was repulsed, and contemporary accounts describe how the Confederate troops spent the night on high ground while many Union soldiers had "to remain in the water all night." Neither side stayed completely dry during this standoff, however, because a heavy rain continued to fall.

By dawn the next day, February 3, some of Mower's forces were attempting to ford the river on either side of the Confederate defenses by constructing two corduroy roads, pathways made of planks laid across logs (several local homes were torn down to supply this lumber). Others spent their time felling cypress trees and using them to cross the river in single file. Both strategies eventually succeeded, and enough Union troops made their way to the other side of the Salkehatchie that the Confederate defenders were outflanked and thus compelled to abandon their position and retreat to Branchville.

In the two days of fighting, both sides lost about one hundred men each, including those who were wounded or captured. With the loss of Rivers Bridge, which has been described as "a heavily fortified and naturally strong position in the middle of a cold and terrible swamp," the road was open to Sherman's advance on Columbia, which fell only two weeks later. The war itself would be over in less than three months.

In 1945, the battlefield site with its well-preserved Confederate earthworks was donated to the state, and it is now heralded as "the only State Historic Site in South Carolina that commemorates the Civil War."

And Beyond

This claim may be open to debate, but what is certainly beyond doubt is the fact that the state's park system has done an exemplary job in interpreting the site for visitors.

Entrance to Rivers Bridge Battlefield. *Michael Budd.*

The battlefield is located near the intersection of Routes 301 and 321 about seven miles southwest of Ehrhardt and thirteen miles east of Allendale. From the parking lot, visitors follow a clearly marked interpretive trail replete with informative markers that tell the story of the battle in both words and pictures. In essence, the trail's topography provides the visitor with a chance to experience both sides of the two-day conflict. It begins at the Confederate breastworks and proceeds down to the river, mirroring the perspective of the defenders whose elevated positions gave them a tactical advantage early on. It concludes along a section of swamp and proceeds up an incline facing the earthen fortifications, providing a glimpse of the difficulties that the Union forces must have faced over 140 years ago.

The state historic site also includes memorial grounds at which ten Confederate casualties are buried: two soldiers from South Carolina, seven from Georgia and one from Arkansas. Although the park itself is open most days year-round, I recommend timing a visit to when the park office is open so that one can purchase the informative guide. For directions and other information, visit the South Carolina State Parks Service on the web at www. SouthCarolinaParks.com.

BARNWELL'S FAMOUS SUNDIAL MARKS MORE THAN TIME

At certain points in our lives, nearly all of us find the occasion to ponder the nature of time and try to fathom the mysteries of its apparently irreversible momentum. To be human is to be time-conscious.

Perhaps this is why people have always been fascinated by instruments constructed to calculate the passage of time. In this regard, we are fortunate in this part of the state to have one of the most unusual timekeeping devices ever made: the vertical sundial in the courthouse square in Barnwell.

Constructed by Charleston ironmonger D.B. Haselton, the metal sundial was presented to the city of Barnwell in 1858 by state senator and local philanthropist Joseph Duncan Allen, who was apparently a devotee of monuments—he erected memorials to his nanny and to one of his dogs.

Unlike most such instruments, which are positioned parallel to the ground, the Barnwell sundial is perpendicular. Along three sides of the placard's square face are marked the hours of the day; in the center, on either side of the gnomon, is a chart that calibrates how many minutes and seconds the viewer must adjust the shadow measurement according to the day of the year. The sundial is said to be most accurate on June 22, when its reading is purportedly off by only two minutes; at other points in the calendar, its reading can be at variance from official Eastern Standard Time by as many as sixteen minutes. A bronze plaque affixed to the back of the concrete curbing that now surrounds the dial provides instructions on how to use this particular timepiece.

Although Captain Allen lost his fortune in the Civil War and much of the city of Barnwell was destroyed by Union forces under the command of Hugh Judson Kilpatrick in 1865, the sundial still survives in its original location. Ironically enough, this device constructed to measure time has itself become a symbol of steadfastness and resilience in spite of time's mutability. As such, it stands as a symbol of the town itself.

It is little wonder, therefore, that when the citizens of Barnwell began to plan for the town's bicentennial it was decided that a fitting memorial to that momentous municipal anniversary might be the refurbishment of its most enduring landmark. Thus, the parking lot that had once abutted the

Barnwell County Courthouse and the vertical sundial. *Michael Budd.*

95

sundial was replaced in 1986 by a circular brick courtyard enclosed by a low brick wall. To show off the sundial to even greater effect, Greenville-based artist Alexandra "Zan" Wells was commissioned to create two freestanding sculptures. One is a little girl, positioned on the pavement below the sundial, gazing upward with a smile on her face. Modeled after the artist's own granddaughter, Mary Ellen Dudash, the young girl holds her sunbonnet behind her back with both hands. Her every feature, from her buckled shoes to the collar on her dress, is meticulously rendered.

The second sculptural piece comes in two complementary parts. First, there is a young barefoot boy who with arms outstretched cheerfully balances on the cement base that surrounds the sundial. On the opposite side of this roughly octagonal pedestal are the two sock-filled shoes that the boy has apparently discarded in his haste to circumnavigate the base of the monument. The sculpture of the little boy is also inspired by a living subject, Chase Ferguson of Warrenville.

Zan Wells arrived at her current profession by a rather circuitous route. The sister of Jasper Johns, one of the most celebrated painters and printmakers of the second half of the twentieth century, and Owen Lee, a noted art educator, Wells has been a homemaker, a potter and a guiding light in women's golf in South Carolina.

Wells herself may very well serve as an object lesson in making the most of one's time. It was not until after her fiftieth birthday that she decided to devote herself exclusively to sculpture. Following attendance at a number of workshops and private study with a veteran sculptor in Arizona, Wells started accepting public commissions, and her work can now be found across the state, including outside the public library in Traveler's Rest, in a hospital garden in Laurens and next to the city hall in Greenville.

To date, however, Wells is most associated with a public art project in Greenville inspired by the classic children's book *Goodnight Moon* by Margaret Wise Brown. On nearly every page of this simple narrative, illustrated by Clement Hurd, there is a mouse, and trying to find all of the mice in the book has amused countless readers since 1947. In fact, this particular imaginary "mouse hunt" eventually inspired Wells to orchestrate a live-action quest on a nine-block stretch of downtown Greenville. Her *Mice on Main* is composed of nine bronze mice sculpted in 2000 and strategically placed to encourage exploration by children and their parents of Greenville's revitalized urban core.

"Lost time is never found again," writes Benjamin Franklin in his classic *Poor Richard's Almanac*. Before another weekend goes by, readers may want to make the trip to Barnwell to see the celebrated sundial, which may

And Beyond

very well be the only example of this particular solar instrument to be found in the United States.

Visitors to Barnwell should also spend some time examining another landmark only one block from the courthouse square: the Church of the Holy Apostles on Patterson Street. Built in 1857, this wood-frame gothic structure is one of the town's few public buildings to survive the fire set by Federal troops in 1865. Local legend asserts that General Kilpatrick's horses were stabled in the building, drank from the baptismal font and left their hoof prints in the wooden flooring. Particularly impressive is the East Window, funded by James Henry Hammond, one of the wealthiest planters and most influential politicians of antebellum South Carolina; his home Redcliffe, near Beech Island, is now a state park.

ARTIST RECEIVES SOUTH CAROLINA'S GREATEST HONOR

What do our state's most popular rock band and most celebrated representational artist have in common? They both have won the Order of the Palmetto, South Carolina's highest civilian honor. Hootie and the Blowfish, the band formed by four University of South Carolina undergraduates in 1986, won their prize for service to the state and nation in 1999; Jim Harrison, an internationally acknowledged chronicler of rural America, received his award in 2009.

Established in 1971, the Order of the Palmetto is modeled after similar distinctions granted by the governors of other states across the country, such as the Honorable Order of Kentucky Colonels and North Carolina's Order of the Longleaf Pine. Harrison's receipt of this honor from Governor Mark Sanford recognizes his thirty-five-year career as a painter, printmaker, illustrator and philanthropist. Represented in personal and corporate collections in both this country and abroad, the artist has given freely of his time and work by granting the use of a number of his now-classic images of a vanishing agrarian South as part of the fundraising campaigns of public institutions, like USC Aiken and South Carolina Educational Television (SCETV).

The genesis of Jim Harrison's remarkable career is familiar to the artist's many admirers. When he was barely a teenager, he landed a summer job as the apprentice to sign painter J.J. Cornforth, who was commissioned by the local Coca-Cola bottling plant to decorate with the soft drink logo the sides of buildings in the area surrounding the crossroads town of Denmark, South Carolina. This early introduction to what Harrison himself has referred to as "the art of lettering" eventually led to his subsequent career as a professional artist.

Harrison continues to maintain a relationship with the Coca-Cola Company. In fact, each year he publishes another calendar in his Coca-Cola series, featuring twelve images of rural structures embellished with the company trademark and arranged to reflect the changing seasons. About this partnership, Harrison has commented, "I jokingly have said that I have worked for Coca-Cola for fifty years, possibly longer than any other employee there." This relationship began with the more than one hundred structures he painted with advertising signs in his days as Cornforth's assistant and continues to this day with the creation of calendars, notecards and both limited and open edition prints and canvas transfers of images featuring the soft drink brand.

Regardless of his commercial and artistic success—his original paintings are regularly featured in exhibitions at such prestigious venues as the Hammer Galleries in New York and the Conacher Galleries in San Francisco—Jim Harrison admits to having a personal mission: to preserve the architectural remnants of our collective past. Because of the relentless "march of progress" and the slow retreat of agricultural America, many of the rural churches, gristmills and covered bridges that Harrison has depicted over the years survive today solely in his paintings or in the photographs from which he often works.

Harrison has taken thousands of photos of places that catch his eye. Given the opportunity, however, he much prefers to work on the spot, starting in the morning and trying to finish in one day. He paints in acrylic, using minute brushstrokes. He will sometimes spend months on the works that are eventually earmarked for reproduction as prints because his patrons, he asserts, are often accustomed to "inspect every dot."

With works that he intends as book illustrations, however, Harrison employs a looser style that photo reduction later tightens up. He has collaborated on a number of volumes—supplying images for someone else's text—but on occasion, he generates both word and picture, as in the case with his study of country stores. This particular volume, published in 1994, required personal research on what Harrison considers the "golden age" of the country store, a period from just after the end of the Civil War to the time of the Great Depression.

And Beyond

The Jim Harrison Gallery. *Michael Budd.*

Along with artists such as Andrew Wyeth, Harrison is a notable exponent of the New Realism introduced in the 1960s. He shares with Wyeth an eye for detail and a penchant for rural scenes and dilapidated structures with their just-abandoned look. Yet, while Wyeth's work concentrates on the bleakness of late autumn and early winter in his native North, Harrison has a richer palette because of the South's warmer, more luxuriant landscape. Imbued with a strong sense of place, Harrison's paintings, at their best, do more than just capture local color. There is a hushed quiet about his settings; each one is a frozen moment that encourages contemplation and a personal relationship with the subject.

Most of his images in more affordable formats are available at his very own gallery in downtown Denmark. Located at the intersection of Routes 78 and 321, the Jim Harrison Gallery is undoubtedly the most significant and most popular landmark in that part of the state.

Housed in a brick building that originally served as a general store from roughly 1910 to 1920, the gallery boasts its original tin ceilings and a dramatic roof lantern, which casts a warm glow over the interior exhibition space. Across the street is Jim Harrison Square. Featuring a central fountain and gazebo, this pleasant exterior space was dedicated to the artist in 1997 by the citizens of Denmark in "grateful appreciation" for his continuing "devotion to his community, its people, and its progress." For more information on the artist and his gallery, visit www.jimharrison.com.

INTEREST IN ROMANTIC NOVELIST REVIVED

During his lifetime, William Gilmore Simms was sometimes touted as America's best novelist. Writing in the tradition of Sir Walter Scott and James Fenimore Cooper, Simms, a Charleston native, produced over thirty novels that combine fictional characters and historical events. His first popular success, the novel *Guy Rivers* (1834), revolves around the dastardly career of a diabolical bandit on the Georgia frontier during the colonial period; his most consistently popular novel, *The Yemassee: A Romance of Carolina* (1835), features a love story set against the backdrop of an early conflict between Native Americans and British colonists in 1715.

By the turn of the twentieth century, however, Simms's literary reputation was on the decline, and it was not until contemporary scholars focused their sights on sectional literature that something akin to a Simms revival was underway. In 1993, the William Gilmore Simms Society was established, and for the last fifteen years, the University of Alabama Press has been publishing new editions of his novels, many of which had long been out of print. Indeed, with the statewide celebration in 2006 of the 200th anniversary of the author's birth, a Simms revival may very well be in the works.

Although the author is most associated with the city of Charleston, where he was born in 1806 and where he died in 1870—this is also where he studied law at the age of eighteen and the site of the *Charleston City Gazette*, a newspaper of which Simms was partial owner for a time—there are other spots across South Carolina that may lay claim to some connection to this early giant of southern literature.

In the Central Savannah River Area, for example, is a site with a significant connection to Simms: Redcliffe Plantation in Beech Island. This restored antebellum mansion was the home of James Henry Hammond, the United States senator most famous for his "Cotton is King" speech. Hammond was also one of Simms's closest friends; the two men corresponded with each other faithfully for nearly twenty-five years. Of their friendship, Simms wrote, "Never were thoughts more intimate than his and mine. We had few or no secrets from each other; we took few steps without mutual consultation. I felt there was something kindred in our intellectual nature. Certainly, there was much, very much in common between us."

Both men, for example, shared an interest in spiritualism and even did some research on mediums; they were also ardent apologists for the southern agrarian system. Simms's own devotion to the plantation lifestyle can be traced to his second marriage; his wife, Chevillette Eliza Roach, was the daughter of a wealthy plantation owner, and she brought to the marriage a dowry that included an estate called Woodlands. After 1836, Simms himself came to divide his residency between his house on Smith Street in Charleston and this plantation located about four miles east of Bamberg. Although the original house was burned down in 1865 either by slaves or by General W.T. Sherman's forces, the property itself is still in family hands.

In fact, the land and its people are the focus of a major ETV-sponsored documentary that was filmed in 2005. Entitled *Shared History*, this motion picture written and produced by Felicia Furman, a direct descendant of William Gilmore Simms, traces the two-hundred-year history of the white and black families that called Woodlands their home. Part of the footage showcases a 1996 reunion between Simms family descendants and the descendants of seventy enslaved people, many of whom stayed on as tenants and sharecroppers following the Civil War.

Simms himself recorded that a number of his former slaves decided to follow Federal troops on their march north and that some made up their minds to resettle in Liberia; those who chose to stay on the land became the focus of one of the most ironic elements of this interesting tale. Right after the war, as an official of the Bureau of Refugees, James Beecher, the brother of novelist Harriet Beecher Stowe, visited Woodlands to take a census of the African Americans who made the decision to remain where they were born and raised.

This visit set the stage for a collision of two radically different worldviews. Earlier, in both his fiction and nonfiction writing, Simms had made it a point to try to contradict the grim picture of slavery presented in *Uncle Tom's Cabin*. In fact, he authored perhaps the most famous of the two dozen so-called "Anti-Tom novels" that appeared after the 1852 publication of Harriet Beecher Stowe's immensely popular abolitionist work. Entitled *The Sword and the Distaff*, Simms's narrative re-created an idealized agrarian society dominated by noble-minded masters who kindly looked after the welfare of innocent, trusting and largely grateful slaves.

Although there is no hard evidence that Beecher ever confronted Simms in the flesh, such an encounter conjures up a host of imaginative possibilities. A missionary to China before the war and an officer in a black cavalry regiment during the conflict, Beecher, who would have been about thirty-eight in 1865–66 when he worked for the Freedmen's Bureau, would have stood in sharp contrast to Simms, the sixty-year-old apologist of a financially and morally bankrupt economic system.

However, the struggle for social justice in America, though often marked by dramatic setbacks, tends ultimately to move in the direction of a general recognition of equal rights for all citizens. Although, as a planter by marriage, he himself adopted the then accepted proprietary attitudes of his class regarding the African American population in their charge, Simms was much more enlightened in his attitude toward Native American people, whom he depicted, at times, almost as sympathetically as his more heralded literary contemporary James Fenimore Cooper.

It was left to his descendants to balance the scales regarding relations between whites and blacks. Today, as the 2005 documentary makes clear, the Simms family still clings to half of the four thousand acres once forcibly cultivated by slaves, but they now recognize the lingering bond between them and the people whom their ancestors once owned. There is a general acknowledgment that the land binds both groups, who now gather periodically to acknowledge their shared history and pave the way for a more equitable collective future.

TRINITY CHURCHYARD
SERVES AS STATE PANTHEON

Stoop, angels, hither from the skies.
There is no holier spot of ground
Than where defeated valor lies,
By mourning beauty crowned!

So reads the last stanza of Henry Timrod's "Ode at Magnolia Cemetery," considered by many scholars to be one of the best poems inspired by the Civil War. Written in 1867 to commemorate the act of decorating the graves of the Confederate dead, whom the poet labels "martyrs of the fallen cause," the ode focuses equal attention on those killed in battle and those who survived to grieve,

The grave site of Henry Timrod. *Tom Mack.*

particularly the women, the "sisters bringing their tears and memorial blooms."

Ironically enough, Timrod himself became the subject of commemorative efforts when in 1901 the Timrod Memorial Association placed a rough-hewn granite boulder with a polished medallion of text on his burial plot in the churchyard of Trinity Cathedral in Columbia. Touted as the "Poet Laureate of the Confederacy," Timrod spent the war years not on the battlefield but at his desk. Although he did try to enlist for active service in the military, his precarious health, particularly his struggle with tuberculosis, limited him to a spectator's role. Still, he consistently supported the war effort with his pen, both as a poet/lyricist and a journalist.

In fact, Henry Timrod was an associate editor of a paper entitled the *South Carolinian* in Columbia when Union forces under the command of General William Tecumseh Sherman invaded the state and much of South Carolina's capital city burned to the ground. Two years later, Timrod died and was buried next to his infant son Willie on the grounds of one of the few important buildings in Columbia to survive the fires of 1865.

Consecrated in 1847 and expanded in 1861–62 during the first years of the Civil War, Trinity Episcopal Church, a cathedral parish since 1977, stands today where it has always stood on Sumter Street, facing the statehouse. Enfolding the north side of the building, enclosed by a brick and iron fence, is one of the most interesting graveyards in our state because it became the final resting place of so many important historical figures.

Among them is Wade Hampton III, who served, coincidentally enough, as a pallbearer during Henry Timrod's interment. Perhaps the most distinguished member of a family long associated with the history of our state—his grandfather was a hero of the American Revolution—Hampton willingly cast aside his responsibilities as South Carolina's wealthiest landowner to enlist in the Confederate military. Despite his personal reservations regarding the dissolution of the Union and the defensibility of slavery, Hampton had a very strong attachment to his home state. During the course of the war, he proved to be one of the very best cavalry officers to serve in either army. The South's defeat, however, meant the ruin of Hampton's fortune; upon his return to South Carolina after the war, he entered politics partially because of the need to earn a living. His election as governor in 1876 ended Reconstruction in South Carolina, and when he died in 1902, twenty thousand mourners surrounded his grave site in Trinity Churchyard.

Wade Hampton III's burial monument, a more elaborate variation on those that house the remains of his forebears, is commonly labeled a "bench tomb" or "grave shed." In essence, the above-ground sarcophagus or stone coffin was originally popularized by both the ancient Greeks and Romans; this particular example features a small Doric column at each corner to hold the inscribed slab that serves as the lid of the marble depository. "Wholehearted, truehearted, faithful and loyal" reads the list of traits ascribed to Hampton on the "roof" of his neoclassical tomb.

Fine examples of other major types of funerary markers designate the final resting places of other notable South Carolinians. Thomas Cooper, an acquaintance of Thomas Jefferson and an early president of what was to become the University of South Carolina, is buried beneath a truncated obelisk whose inscription calls attention to his two doctorates. The Romans first used as a memorial this shortened variation on the original Egyptian form.

Close by the monument to Dr. Cooper is a broken cylindrical column on whose fractured top a carved laurel wreath rests askew; this stone memorial, emblematic of a life cut short, marks the grave of States Rights Gist, whose first name calls attention to his family's political stance—he had a brother named Independent. Gist, a native of Union, South Carolina, and a graduate of South Carolina College (as USC was then known), was one of six Confederate generals killed in action on a single day during the Battle of Franklin in Tennessee in the fall of 1864. On one side of the base of this memorial, it reads: "He fulfilled the hero's and the patriot's part," and for once, this sentiment seems not to be an exaggeration: Gist was shot in the chest while leading a charge on foot against a Union fortified position.

The grave site of Wade Hampton III. *Tom Mack.*

A stroll through the churchyard at Trinity Cathedral in Columbia is like tracing the history of our state; each monument provides both verbal and visual text to aid in the interpretation of those past events that have shaped our collective present.

SOUTH CAROLINA RETAINS TIES TO CONFEDERATE DIARIST

From her home in Columbia, Mary Boykin Chesnut listened with growing alarm to the news of the advance of Union forces under General William Tecumseh Sherman. "He has left a track as bare and blackened as a fire leaves on the prairies," she wrote in her journal in February 1865. "Can we check or impede his march? Can anyone?"

The answers to those questions soon became clear as Sherman's troops entered, without serious impediment, South Carolina's capital city, half of which would soon be burned to the ground.

Having fled a few days earlier by train to North Carolina, Mary Chesnut was not present to witness the city's tragic fate, although she had been on the spot during many of the most dramatic moments of the Civil War. Indeed, most historians agree that the journal of this South Carolina native provides the best record of the social climate of the South during that turbulent period.

Published in 1905 and 1949 in highly bowdlerized editions under the title *A Diary from Dixie*, Chesnut's candid account of the war years was finally given its due in a more complete and uncensored version in 1982. Edited by C. Vann Woodward, this particular volume entitled *Mary Chesnut's Civil War* won the coveted Pulitzer Prize in History for that year.

Born in 1823, Mary Chesnut grew up in privileged circumstances. Her father, Stephen Decatur Miller, was, in succession, a United States congressman, senator and South Carolina governor. When she married James Chesnut in 1840, Mary aligned herself with one of the largest landowning families in the state and with one of South Carolina's rising political stars. James Chesnut was elected a United States senator in 1858, and Mary joined him in Washington, D.C., where they made personal and professional connections that were to determine their future when the country broke apart in 1861. Of particular significance was the fact that they developed a close friendship with both Jefferson and Varina Davis.

After the election of Abraham Lincoln, the Chesnuts returned to South Carolina, where James participated in the drafting of the ordinance of secession. This was the beginning of their life at the epicenter of the rise and fall of the Confederate states. They were, for instance, in Charleston for the surrender of Fort Sumter in April 1861; indeed, James Chesnut served as an aide-de-camp to the leader of the besieging Confederate forces, General P.G.T. Beauregard. They traveled to Montgomery, Alabama, and Richmond, Virginia, in the furtherance of James Chesnut's work in the Confederate cabinet; he rose to the rank of brigadier general largely as a result of his services to the government.

As members of the inner circle, the Chesnuts were often in the right place at the right time, and Mary Chesnut kept meticulous journals to record her thoughts and experiences from February 1861 to July 1865, when the Chesnuts returned to their beloved Mulberry Plantation outside of Camden to discover that Union soldiers had pillaged the property. In the last twenty years of her life before her death at the age of sixty-three in 1886, she revised her journal entries out of a personal presentiment that one day her words would be of value in conjuring up images of a lost society. She left all fifty notebooks to a friend, who kept them under an armoire in her bedroom until they finally saw the light of day in the abridged 1905 edition.

And Beyond

Mary Chesnut's work continues to fascinate today's readers not only because of the fact that she was on the scene when history happened but also because of her extraordinarily advanced views on gender and race matters. She was, for one thing, a very outspoken feminist in the context of her time; although she benefited economically from the plantation system, she was personally averse to slavery as an institution.

Readers of her work may be happy to know that four of the family properties in and around Camden—Mulberry, Sarsfield, Bloomsbury and Kamschatka—still exist in private hands. Mulberry is, in fact, owned by Chesnut descendants, and both James and Mary are buried in the family plot on Knight's Hill in Camden.

For those who would like a closer look at a place that Mary Chesnut knew well, it is even possible to spend the night in the cottage that the Chesnuts called home in the city of Columbia, a residence that they used when the countryside became less and less secure as the war progressed. Built about 1850 on Hampton Street, diagonally across from the house where Woodrow Wilson was to spend his teenaged years, the Chesnut Cottage is now operated as a bed-and-breakfast establishment.

Chesnut Cottage. *Michael Budd.*

Interestingly enough, this one-and-a-half story, white frame structure was the setting of a speech given by President Jefferson Davis to the citizens of Columbia. He spoke from the front porch to an assembled crowd in October 1864 when he was visiting the city. According to innkeeper Gale Garrett, Mary Chesnut sat in one of the front rooms to listen through an open window to Davis while he addressed the gathering on the street from the porch.

That particular room, now named after Jefferson Davis, is one of three guest rooms in the main house along with two in the refurbished carriage house. Each room is furnished with period antiques; the Davis room, for example, boasts of a trunk said to have been used by Alexander Stephens, vice-president of the Confederacy—his plantation outside of Crawfordville, Georgia, is now a house museum. Volumes from an extensive library of works related to the Civil War can be found throughout the cottage, and the back porch has been enclosed to create a sunny breakfast room.

For those interested in learning more about Mary Boykin Chesnut, the best start would be reading the one-volume edition of her journals *Mary Chesnut's Civil War*, edited by C. Vann Woodward. Also recommended is the definitive biography by Elisabeth Muhlenfeld.

STATEHOUSE MONUMENTS OFFER STORIES IN STONE

On the eighteen landscaped acres that surround the statehouse complex in Columbia are nearly thirty public monuments. Some, like the General Wade Hampton Monument, celebrate the individual lives of noteworthy South Carolinians; others, like the African American History Monument, commemorate the contributions of particular groups of people to the development of our state and nation.

I have strolled through the manicured grounds of the seven-building capitol complex a number of times to take a closer look at the monuments that the citizens of our state have erected near the seat of government. Nearly all of these memorials tell interesting stories, and a few may hold surprises for the casual visitor.

Consider, for example, the Spanish-American War Monument on the Gervais Street side of the statehouse. This particular memorial is noteworthy not only for its intention but also for its sculptor. On a stone pedestal stands a

Ruggles Kitson's *The Hiker. Michael Budd.*

bronze "rough rider" holding a rifle horizontally across the front of his body; he sports a broad-brimmed hat, a cartridge belt around his waist and knee boots. He appears to be the embodiment of the American foot soldier who fought in Cuba and the Philippines in aid of the native inhabitants in their struggle to overthrow their Spanish overlords.

Called *The Hiker*, this six-foot-tall figurative sculpture is one of fifty-two casts scattered about the country, all by one of the few American women to make a career of sculpting public monuments before the twentieth century.

Born in 1876, Theo Alice Ruggles Kitson began her art studies under the tutelage of her guardian and future husband, sculptor Henry Hudson Kitson, when she was only in her teens. Before the age of twenty, she was already earning praise in the annual exhibitions or "salons" of the French Royal Academy of Painting and Sculpture. After she separated from her husband in 1919, Ruggles Kitson, as she is popularly known, operated her own studio in Massachusetts until her death in 1932. Her most noteworthy accomplishment is the seventy portrait busts of Confederate and Union generals that adorn the Vicksburg Civil War Memorial.

On the base of this particular monument in Columbia are three quotes from noted military leaders in the Spanish-American War, including a once-famous line attributed to Commodore Dewey. During the Battle of Manila Bay in 1898, he is reputed to have called out to the captain of the USS *Olympia*, the flagship of the Asiatic Squadron: "Fire when you are ready, Gridley." Charles Vernon Gridley did indeed order the firing of the ship's guns, and he stayed on the bridge despite ill health—he was to die of cancer only one month later—to witness the American naval victory.

Not far from Kitson's *Hiker*, on the corner of Gervais and Sumter Streets in a cobblestone, hedge-framed courtyard, is the James F. Byrnes Monument, a larger version of the statue that can be found in front of the Aiken County Courthouse. This piece is one of over five hundred different sculptures created by Delaware artist Charles Parks, whose Brandywine River studio was showcased in a 1999 video documentary produced by Teleduction. This full-scale version of the Byrnes Monument on the statehouse grounds has one advantage over its Aiken counterpart, and that is the additional visual information that greater size makes possible. In both versions of the piece, Byrnes—who was a congressman, senator, governor, Supreme Court justice, "Assistant President" under Franklin Roosevelt and secretary of state under Harry Truman—sits in his judicial robes with both hands holding a closed book. Only in the larger version, however, is it possible for the sculptor to carve a title on the bronze volume: "All in One Life," a reference to the Aiken resident's extraordinary career resume and, I think, justification for a statement carved on one side of the memorial's base: "the most distinguished South Carolinian of his lifetime."

Another personal discovery made during one of my strolls across the statehouse grounds concerns the Strom Thurmond Monument opposite the Pendleton Street entrance to the statehouse. In this 1999 sculpture fashioned by North Carolina artist William Frederick Behrends, Senator Thurmond, looking as he did in middle age, strides confidently forward.

The Strom Thurmond Monument. *Tom Mack.*

Because of revelations made after Thurmond's death, however, the text on the stone plinth required some amendment. The final item on Thurmond's extensive curriculum vitae had to be recarved, and the number of his children increased from four to five to include his mixed-race child Essie Mae Washington-Williams. The name "Essie Mae" was added below the names of the four children of his second marriage—his first wife was Jean Crouch

The J. Marion Sims Monument. *Michael Budd.*

and his second, Nancy Moore. Long before that first marriage, when he was in his early twenties, Thurmond had relations with the family maid, Carrie Butler, then only sixteen, and she bore him a child. This extra carving at the bottom of his extensive stone resume is a belated but appropriate public acknowledgment of a paternity kept secret for seven decades.

Another monument that may yet require some revision is the memorial dedicated to a now-controversial nineteenth-century physician, J. Marion Sims, who is sometimes called the "father of gynecology." A native of Lancaster, South Carolina, Sims developed various surgical techniques for the treatment of gynecological disorders, and he is credited with the invention of a number of surgical instruments, including the first speculum. The present monument, erected in 1929 on the corner of Gervais and Assembly Streets, speaks of how Sims "died with the benediction of mankind."

That assertion, however, has raised eyebrows in the last thirty years. While it is certainly true that he made a significant contribution to medical science, particularly in the area of women's reproductive health, Sims has been the focus of contemporary criticism because of the time he spent in Alabama in the 1840s, experimenting on female slaves in an effort to perfect his procedures— one unfortunate woman was the subject of over thirty operations. Despite what his statehouse monument may proclaim about his achievements as "the first surgeon of the ages in ministry to women," today's jury is still out on Dr. Sims.

For anyone planning a trip to Columbia to tour the statehouse and its extensive grounds, I recommend picking up the twelve-page guide published by the South Carolina Department of Parks, Recreation and Tourism. Entitled *A Walk through History*, the brochure contains a helpful map.

NATIONAL PARK COMMEMORATES REVOLUTIONARY WAR'S LONGEST SIEGE

In the heat of summer in 1781, the longest siege of the American Revolution took place in South Carolina. General Nathaniel Greene and a Patriot army of a little over 1,000 men surrounded the frontier outpost of Ninety Six garrisoned by a force of 550 Americans still loyal to the British Crown.

Established as a major center of trade with the surrounding Indian population and named probably for the fact that it was exactly ninety-six miles south of the major Cherokee town of Keowee, Ninety Six was heavily fortified. On one side of the small settlement was a stockade fort; on the other side was a star fort, so-called because its fourteen-foot-tall earthen walls were constructed to form an eight-pointed star.

It was the latter fortification that proved too much for the besieging Patriot army. Although a force under the command of Virginian "Light Horse

Harry" Lee took the timber fort on one side of the town, the walls of the
star fort proved too high and the defenders too determined for Greene to
take the earthen redoubt. He ended the twenty-eight-day siege when news
reached him that a British relief force was on its way from Charleston—
called Charles Town at that time.

One theory about why the Loyalist or Tory defenders of Ninety Six fought
so doggedly involves the fear of retribution. As Walter Edgar points out in
his history of South Carolina, some of the bloodiest sectarian violence of
the whole war took place in the backcountry, where "indiscriminate murder
and looting" were commonplace on both sides. Many of those still loyal to
the Crown must surely have feared what might happen to them if they ever
fell into the hands of Patriots or partisans who still harbored resentment for
atrocities committed by their Tory neighbors.

This strategic withdrawal, however, proved to be a victory of sorts
because the British reinforcements stayed in Ninety Six only long enough
to destroy the fortifications and evacuate the local Loyalist population, who
chose to accompany the British military back to Charles Town. With the loss
of the principal fortified outpost in the upcountry, the British occupation
thenceforth became limited to the coastal area, where soldiers had increasing
difficulty in provisioning their forces and diminished opportunity to rally
civilian support.

Most of the site of Old Ninety Six lay undisturbed for two hundred years
until archaeologists focused their attention on the star fort. In 1973 and 1974,
they restored the old siege trenches designed by Polish-Lithuanian Patriot
and American ally Thaddeus Kosciusko, who was well versed in European
methods of siege craft.

Amazingly enough, today's visitors to Ninety Six National Historic Site
can follow the physical progress of the original siege. The current footpath
starts from the first trench dug by Greene's men through all the subsequent
trenches that zigzag two hundred yards between the site of the Patriot camp
and the fort. The trenches end at the entrance to the tunnel dug by the edge
of the wall; it was here that Kosciusko himself was wounded by a bayonet-
wielding Loyalist defender, part of a group sent out from the star fort to
impede the progress of the siege.

One of a host of fascinating European volunteers in our country's fight
for freedom, Kosciusko eventually became an international symbol of the
struggle against tyranny. For his seven years of service as a military engineer,
the Continental Congress granted him citizenship and a parcel of land,
which he intended to be sold to fund the emancipation and education of

enslaved people. Kosciusko eventually returned to Europe, where he fought against Russian occupation of his native land.

On one particular summer visit to Old Ninety Six, I found it very easy to identify with members of Greene's army as they engaged in their patient but exhausting labor. The intense heat of a June day in South Carolina is the same now as it was over two hundred years ago. The mosquitoes are still omnipresent, although they must have plagued Greene's men to a greater extent than they did me since I was armed with a modern bug repellent. All that was missing was the sound of cannon fire.

The one-mile walking tour of the park takes visitors past the trenches and the ten-foot-tall reconstruction of a Patriot rifle tower into the center of what remains of the star fort. There one proceeds along the communication trench to the site of the town and onward to the stockade fort, which has been reconstructed.

All visits to Old Ninety Six should begin in the modern visitor center, where one can see a short video about the history of the place and examine artifacts excavated at the site. For more information on the park, located about two miles south of the present-day town of Ninety Six, which is just a few miles outside of Greenwood, South Carolina, visit the National Park Service on the web at www.nps.gov/nisi.

BURT-STARK MANSION RECALLS END OF CIVIL WAR

As he sat in his customary pew at Saint Paul's Church just one block from the statehouse in Richmond, Virginia, on April 2, 1865, Jefferson Davis had a difficult time focusing on the Episcopalian liturgy. His attention was diverted by the delivery of a message from Robert E. Lee, who wanted to advise the president of the Confederacy that the city could no longer be defended.

Davis left the church for a meeting with his cabinet, and at the conclusion of that session, he departed that same day by train for Danville; there he and his party remained for a few days before heading for Greensboro, North Carolina, and then to Charlotte, where he heard the news of Abraham Lincoln's assassination. Eventually, Jefferson Davis arrived in Abbeville, South Carolina.

Commentators disagree as to the full purpose of the Confederate president's movements after the fall of Richmond and Lee's subsequent

The Burt-Stark Mansion. *Michael Budd.*

surrender at Appomattox Court House on April 9. Some assert that he hoped eventually to reach Texas to rally whatever Confederate forces might be willing to continue the struggle until the most favorable surrender terms could be negotiated with the United States government.

And Beyond

The reason that he spent a night in Abbeville, however, seems not to be a matter of conjecture. While her husband was making slower progress south due to his official responsibilities, Varina Davis, first lady of the Confederacy, had been sent ahead for her own safety. During her flight, she sought refuge for ten days at the home of Armistead Burt in Abbeville. Burt, a former member of the United States Congress, and his wife Martha were good friends of the Davis family.

On May 2, 1865, Davis himself arrived in Abbeville and spent a rainy night at the Burt home. During his relatively brief time in the two-story, Greek Revival mansion, it is said that he called a meeting of the cabinet members and chief military staff in his party. Their agenda focused, of course, on the final conduct of the war. During this session, Davis asserted his desire to figure out ways to continue the fighting, but the four cabinet members and five brigade commanders in attendance argued that further resistance was futile. Davis is said to have responded to their advice, "All is indeed lost."

The house itself, renamed the Burt-Stark Mansion in honor of both families that served as its principal residents, still seems imbued with the atmosphere of that dramatic period in history. The parlor to the left of the main entrance boasts a set of upholstered chairs and footstools that are said to have been used during the war council held in the mansion; in the second-floor hallway is a desk owned by Armistead Burt and perhaps used by Davis; and on the second floor is also the bedroom, the second on the left as one ascends the stairs, where Davis spent the night—it still has the original four-poster bed.

The bedroom itself faces the front of the house, whose entrance grounds are triangular in shape, formed by the intersection of two roads that merge just north of Abbeville's famous town square. It is easy to imagine that for a brief period the space must have seemed a pleasant sanctuary for a man hunted far and wide. Indeed, only eight days later, on May 10, Davis, who had been reunited with his wife and four children in southern Georgia, was captured by the Fourth Michigan Cavalry near the town of Irwinsville.

For additional information, visit the mansion on the web at www.burt-stark.com.

ABBEVILLE PAINTINGS
PRESERVE MOMENTS OF SOUTHERN PAST

One of the most significant artist-historians of the Old South was actually a self-confessed "transplanted Yankee." Born in 1882 in Illinois and raised in Indiana, Wilbur G. Kurtz didn't actually venture south until he was twenty-one and doing research on Andrews's raiders, a group of out-of-uniform Union soldiers, who hijacked a Confederate locomotive with the intention of destroying train rails and bridges between Atlanta and Chattanooga in 1862. Although the mission ended in failure and Andrews and some of his men were eventually captured and hanged, the boldness of the venture captured the collective imagination of the nation during and after the war.

Kurtz visited Atlanta in 1903 with the intention of interviewing survivors of the raid. A graduate of the Art Institute of Chicago, Kurtz was a professional illustrator interested in historical subjects. What he learned during his first trip to the South proved immediately useful; he interviewed six members of the Union raiding party and five Southern pursuers and incorporated their recollections in several accounts that he wrote of the dramatic raid. Many years later, he also served as a technical advisor for the 1956 film *The Great Locomotive Chase*, starring Fess Parker as James Andrews.

Kurtz also discovered in that 1903 trip that he really liked what he called the "quiet, pleasant town of Atlanta where they rolled up the sidewalks at dark every night." Kurtz moved to his new home in 1912, and for the next fifty-five years, he lived in a city so fixated on the future that it often ignored its past.

Yet, it was the region's rich heritage that drew Kurtz to the South in the first place, and he gradually developed a reputation as a painter of meticulously researched images of previously unrecorded history, not just of the Atlanta area but of the region as a whole. In addition to his 1934–36 restoration work on the famous Cyclorama of the Battle of Atlanta in Grant Park, Kurtz is best remembered for his 1937–39 service as official "historian" of the film production of *Gone with the Wind*.

Visitors to the Margaret Mitchell House and Museum in Atlanta will find ample evidence of his role in that project. In addition to the apartment at which Mitchell wrote her Pulitzer Prize–winning novel from 1925 to 1932, the site includes the Gone with the Wind Museum, which opened in 1999, the sixtieth anniversary of the film's premiere. Among the preserved memorabilia are many objects collected by Kurtz himself. Some are related to his official role as consultant, including a small container of red clay from Clayton County, Georgia, dug up by Kurtz to show the Hollywood producers how the soil should look in the plantation scenes (the film was shot largely in California); some objects betray Kurtz's occasional star-struck moments, including a cigar that he picked up on the set after it was left behind by Clark Gable.

Georgia history, however, was not the only focus of Kurtz's interest. In fact, he created five large-scale paintings that feature significant events and figures in South Carolina's past. Completed in 1922, the five works were commissioned by officials of the Bank of Abbeville to grace their home office on the city's main square. When the bank was eventually bought out by the Bank of America, the building was deeded to the city for use as a welcome center.

Anyone planning a day trip to Abbeville to visit the city's historic sites, do some shopping or attend a performance at the famous opera house should make sure to spend some time in the welcome center to examine the Kurtz paintings.

In chronology, the first work depicts General Andrew Pickens on a white horse, pausing before the fortified Block House, which he built out of logs east of the town square as a sanctuary for women and children in case of an Indian attack. Pickens was a notable militia leader during both the Cherokee War and the American Revolution; in the latter conflict, he led a band of partisans or "regulators" who were "paid in plunder taken from Loyalists."

The second painting marks a more settled period in the town's history: sometime in the 1830s or 1840s, when John C. Calhoun, a planter and practicing attorney in the Abbeville area, was at home from Washington, touching base with his constituents. Calhoun, who served as a U.S. congressman and senator as well as vice president under both John Quincy Adams and Andrew Jackson, was a towering figure in state and national politics before the Civil War.

The third and fourth paintings in the series acknowledge the town's part in the tumultuous period of the War Between the States. One image depicts Judge A.G. McGrath of Charleston addressing an audience of townspeople from a platform constructed on a hill near the main square on November 22, 1860. The principal speaker at this mass rally in support of secession, McGrath is joined onstage by General M.L. Bonham and Major Armistead Burt. The latter notable owned a large house, now a museum, which served as the setting for perhaps the most dramatic event to occur in Abbeville, the last war council of the Confederacy.

In Kurtz's rendering of that particular scene, Jefferson Davis stands in the parlor of the Burt-Stark Mansion, one stop on his flight southward after the

Last Meeting of the War Cabinet by Wilbur Kurtz. *Michael Budd.*

fall of Richmond; seated on either side of him on May 2, 1865, are some of his cabinet ministers, including Secretary of State Judah P. Benjamin and members of his military escort, including General Braxton Bragg, captured in the subdued light of candlesticks and oil lamps.

The fifth and final painting commemorates the establishment of the Bank of Abbeville during Reconstruction. Three of the bank's founders stand in the square; the building that now houses the welcome center is framed behind them.

For more information on Kurtz and his lifelong devotion to southern history, one can visit the Welcome Center in Abbeville, the Margaret Mitchell House and Museum or the Atlanta Historical Society, which houses an extensive collection of his work. Reproductions of many of his images can also be found in the 1969 volume entitled *Atlanta and the Old South: Paintings and Drawings by Wilbur G. Kurtz.*

And Beyond

ANTEBELLUM CHARLESTON MANSION HAS AIKEN TIES

In Charleston, a city noted for its many places of cultural interest, there is one particular landmark with special ties to the history of Aiken. I am referring to the Aiken-Rhett House, now run by the Historic Charleston Foundation as a public museum but once the home for almost 150 years of a family closely connected with the town that bears its name.

Regarded as one of the grandest urban mansions in the country, the house was purchased initially as rental property in 1827 by William Aiken Sr., an Irish immigrant who eventually became the first president of the South Carolina Canal and Railroad Company and, coincidentally, the namesake of the city of Aiken. William Aiken died in a carriage accident in 1831—it is said that his horse became frightened, ironically enough, by the sound of a train whistle—and probably never visited the quiet country crossroads that would eventually bear his name after municipal incorporation in 1835.

Aiken's only son, also named William, moved into the house with his new bride Harriet Lowndes Aiken in 1833 after they decided to make it their permanent residence. For the next twenty years, the ambitious couple made alterations to the property, moving the front entrance to the Elizabeth Street side of the house and adding a large addition to the original building in order to accommodate an art gallery to house works that they purchased on a grand tour of Europe.

William Aiken Jr. was a successful planter and businessman; he served a number of years in both houses of the state legislature and a single term as governor. Because of its owner's prominence in the life of his city and state, the house bore witness to a number of significant events. In 1863, for example, Jefferson Davis spent a week as a guest in the house during an official visit to the city; his approval of the servants' "automatic, noiseless perfection of training" is recorded in the famous *Diary from Dixie* by Mary Boykin Chesnut. In 1864, General Pierre Beauregard, commander of Confederate forces in Charleston, occupied the house as his headquarters partially because of its size and partially because of its location—its distance from the Battery put it out of the range of Union shelling. After Charleston fell to Federal troops in 1865, the house became the target of looters.

Yet, despite the vicissitudes of fortune, many items of furniture and artwork original to the property still remain. Family descendants lived in the house until 1975. Because many of the rooms were closed off to avoid the expense of upkeep, the estate, which has been described as a "time capsule,"

The Aiken-Rhett House. *Michael Budd.*

survived largely unchanged from its 1858 configuration. It is this sense of walking into a space that remains unaltered despite the march of time that the Historic Charleston Foundation has hoped to offer the visitor since the organization acquired the property in 1995.

And Beyond

All visits to the three-story brick townhouse today begin in the entrance hall remodeled on a grand scale in the 1830s, but instead of ascending one of the two marble staircases framed with elaborate wrought-iron railings, one descends to the cavernous storage rooms below ground that now house the gift shop and where one can pay the admission fee and acquire audio headsets for a self-paced tour with taped commentary.

Like so many antebellum sites in the American South, the Aiken-Rhett House has been the subject of much recent research to bring to light not only the day-to-day habits of its owners but also the working conditions of the enslaved population that made the family's opulent lifestyle possible. In this regard, the property is a prime example of what is termed an "urban plantation," and before inspecting the Aiken residence itself, today's visitor is ushered out into the expansive courtyard behind the house, bracketed by two-story buildings, one containing the kitchen and laundry and the other, the stables and carriage house. On the second floor, above these workspaces, are the dormitory-style living quarters of the family's servants, which varied in number from ten to twenty in the years before the Civil War.

In the courtyard, one is asked to imagine the arrival of the family carriage through the gates at the rear of the property as it proceeded through the avenue of magnolia trees, five on a side, and up to the rear of the main house. Therein the lavish tastes of the Aiken and Rhett families—William Aiken Jr.'s daughter, Henrietta, married Major Burnett Rhett—stand in stark contrast to the simple, utilitarian spaces inhabited by the enslaved workers. Upstairs are spacious, specialized living spaces such as dressing rooms, a ballroom and a library with elaborate ornamental moldings, French chandeliers and sculpture while downstairs and in the outbuildings are modest, all-purpose rooms wherein whole families ate, slept and lived their lives.

For more information on the Aiken-Rhett House, visit the Historic Charleston Foundation on the web at www.historiccharleston.org.

Bibliography

Abrams, M.H. *The Mirror and the Lamp.* New York: Oxford University Press, 1971.

Bleser, Carol. *The Hammonds of Redcliffe.* New York: Oxford University Press, 1981.

Bull, Emily. *Eulalie.* Aiken, SC: Kalmia Press, 1973.

Byrnes, James F. *Speaking Frankly.* New York: Harper and Brothers, 1947.

Caldwell, Erskine. *God's Little Acre.* 1933. Athens: University of Georgia Press, 1995.

———. *Tobacco Road.* 1932. Athens: University of Georgia Press, 1995.

Caldwell, Erskine, and Margaret Bourke-White. *You Have Seen Their Faces.* 1937. Athens: University of Georgia Press, 1995.

Cashin, Edward J. *The Brightest Arm of the Savannah: The Augusta Canal 1845–2000.* Augusta, GA: Augusta Canal Authority, 2002.

Charles O. Perry. Darien, CT: DeCesare Design Associates, 1987. Private copy.

Davis, Curtis Carroll. *That Ambitious Mr. Legare: The Life of James M. Legare of South Carolina, Including a Collected Edition of His Verse.* Columbia: University of South Carolina Press, 1971.

Doctorow, E.L. *The March.* New York: Random House, 2005.

Edgar, Walter. *South Carolina: A History.* Columbia: University of South Carolina Press, 1998.

Epps, Edwin. C. *Literary South Carolina.* Spartanburg, SC: Hub City, 2004.

Graydon, Nell, and Margaret Sizemore. *The Amazing Marriage of Marie Eustis and Josef Hofmann.* Columbia: University of South Carolina Press, 1965.

Harper, Francis, ed. *Travels of William Bartram: Naturalist's Edition.* Athens: University of Georgia Press, 1998.

Harrison, Jim. *Country Stores.* Atlanta, GA: Longstreet Press, 1993.

Hofmann, Josef. *Piano Playing with Piano Questions Answered.* Philadelphia: Theodore Presser, 1920.

Koverman, Jill, ed. *"I made this jar": The Life and Works of the Enslaved African-American Potter, Dave.* Columbia, SC: McKissick Museum, 1998.

Kurtz, Wilbur G. *Atlanta and the Old South: Paintings and Drawings by Wilbur G. Kurtz.* Atlanta: American Lithograph Co., 1969.

Lewis, Elizabeth Wittenmyer. *Queen of the Confederacy: The Innocent Deceits of Lucy Holcombe Pickens.* Denton: University of North Texas Press, 2002.

Marling, Karal. *Wall-to-Wall America.* Minneapolis: University of Minnesota Press, 1982.

Muhlenfeld, Elizabeth. *Mary Boykin Chesnut: A Biography.* Baton Rouge: Louisiana State University Press, 1981.

Parks, Edd Winfield, and Aileen W. Parks, eds. *The Collected Poems of Henry Timrod: A Variorum Edition.* Athens: University of Georgia Press, 2007.

Simms, William Gilmore. *Guy Rivers.* 1834. Fayetteville: University of Arkansas Press, 1993

———. *The Sword and the Distaff.* Philadelphia, PA: Lippincott, 1852.

———. *Yemassee.* 1835. Fayetteville: University of Arkansas Press, 1993.

Smith, Gregory White, and Steven Naifeh. *On a Street Called Easy, In a Cottage Called Joye.* Boston: Little, Brown, 1996.

Swensson, Lise, and Nancy Higgins, eds. *New Deal Art in South Carolina.* Columbia: South Carolina State Museum, 1990.

Swinburne, Algernon Charles. *Atalanta in Calydon: A Tragedy.* London: E. Moxon, 1865.

Woodward, C. Vann, ed. *Mary Chesnut's Civil War.* New Haven, CT: Yale University Press, 1981.

Woolsey, Gamel. *Malaga Burning.* Reston, VA: Pythia Press, 1998.

———. *One Way of Love.* New York: Penguin, 1987.

Yerby, Frank. *The Dahomean.* New York: Dial Press, 1971.

———. *A Darkness at Ingraham's Crest.* New York: Dial Press, 1979.

About the Author

Dr. Tom Mack. *Scott Webster.*

Tom Mack has been a member of the faculty of the University of South Carolina–Aiken since 1976. During that time, he has established an enviable "record of teaching excellence as well as outstanding performance in research and public service" for which the USC Board of Trustees named him a Carolina Trustee Professor in 2008. He currently holds the G.L. Toole Chair in English.

Over the years, Dr. Mack has written extensively about American literature and American cultural history. Furthermore, since 1990, he has contributed a weekly column to the *Aiken Standard* on a wide range of topics in the humanities. He is also the founding editor of the *Oswald Review*, an international journal of undergraduate research in the discipline of English.

In 2009, Tom Mack was elected chairman of the Board of Governors of the South Carolina Academy of Authors, an organization responsible for the supervision of the state's literary hall of fame.

Visit us at
www.historypress.net